The 5 Year Plan

Helping you do what you have always wanted to do.

James Mills

www.the5yearplan.co.uk

info@the5yearplan.co.uk
www.the5yearplan.co.uk

Cover and formatting by Gareth Bourne.

First printing 2010

ISBN 978-1-4452-5012-0

What is the one thing you have always wanted to do, could still do, but have not done?

Contents

Part 3: Making It Happen

Epilogue:

Interesting Resources

We must become the change we want to see.

— *Mahatma Ghandi*

Acknowledgements

Writing a book; something I've always wanted to do, has in many ways been an incredible personal journey. For something that I assumed would be an extremely individualistic task I have found that there have been an amazing number of people involved with this process; both directly and indirectly.

Firstly I'll start off by thanking all my friends; quite simply an amazing group of people. In particular I wanted to thank; Gareth (for constant encouragement as well as working his magic on the cover and formatting), Ian (for suggesting the self-publishing route and lulu site), Shona (with whom a conversation sparked the idea for this book - I think!), Lesley (for the appropriate balance of encouragement and challenge), Jack (for hosting those Monday evening book writing sessions when I first seriously considered writing a book) and Kristie (for some really useful discussions around values). I'd also like to thank my family for putting up with my not so social behaviour last Christmas as I came close to completing the book. Secondly there are the people that have coached and mentored me over the past few years; pushing me to pursue a dream that started years ago. In particular I'd like to thank Jean (for challenging me to pursue this dream), Rob (for his support in my big move to London as well as leading by example) and Chris (for his very recent support in the final stretch of this journey).

Thirdly there are also a variety of groups who have been a fantastic support. In particular all the members of London Corinthians who continue to inspire, inform and entertain me on a regular basis. I'd also like to thank the members of West Life Coaching (Simon, Liz, Joanna, Rumy, Kate and Dav) for monthly meetings of fun and learning. Then there is also the 'TC8+1' group (Armando, David, Jake, James, Pinder, Tess, Karina and Jocelyn) who have also been fantastic support in the short time I have known them.

Finally I wanted to thank my colleagues, volunteers, teachers and young people that I have had the pleasure to work with in my 'day job' at Young Enterprise London.

As a result of all the people I interact with I find each day is packed full of challenge, variety and satisfaction; helping me to grow and continually strive to become the best I can be.

James Mills, April 2010

Reading is to the mind what exercise is to the body.

— Joseph Addison

Introduction:
Why read this book?

No matter who we are or where we come from there are two inevitabilities in life that will affect us all as mortal human beings; ageing and death. Time is precious and once spent it can never be reclaimed. Regardless of how much you reminisce, moan or complain, these two inevitabilities will still be there. You have only one shot at this life and so I feel it is appropriate to explain why you should even entertain the idea of working your way through this book.

Yes, I did say work your way through this book and not read. I can absolutely 100% guarantee that reading this book will NOT change your life. What I can assure you is that taking the time to seriously consider the ideas in the book as well as completing the exercises to write your own 5 Year Plan will change your perspective of life and what you get out of it.

The term '5 Year Plan' is often thrown about almost as a cliché. A common interview question, it is considered one of those things that you 'should' have, but is one of those things many people don't have. Therefore it is comparable to regular exercise and a healthy diet. These are two basic things that are proven to help improve the longevity and quality of life, yet are not pursued by a significant number of people. I have also noticed from speaking to friends that the subject of life-planning is one that people feel slightly awkward and uncomfortable discussing. For this very reason I am guessing that if you have started reading this book you are someone that has thought about the idea, but hasn't done it. If this is the case you will be pleased to know that many people are like you.

Having said this, there may be successful people that you admire for achieving what they set out to achieve. Successful people and organisations will have a written plan or list of goals of some description. When I use the word 'success' I leave the definition up to you as I believe we should all have our own definition of this word in line with our values and beliefs. For you it may be material wealth, a high-powered career, education, family, community service or pure hedonism; the list goes on, but the point is that you own your definition of success.

We will explore why people do and don't have a 5 Year Plan later, but I felt the best way to explain why I feel you should have a 5 Year Plan is by telling the story of my experiences of creating my own 5 Year Plans.

My story

I wrote my first 5 Year Plan when I was 19 and believe it was one of the most significant things that I have done in my life. I was coming to the end of a gap year placement before university and collecting my learning points from the experience. I had been working in Graduate Recruitment for a Multinational Energy Generator and had recognised the huge amount of opportunity ahead of me at university. I wanted to make the most of it from both a personal and a professional point of view.

The firm I was working for was undergoing significant organisational change; morale was not at its highest and productivity was equally low. This low tempo environment gave me the freedom to invest time to put together a plan of what I wanted to achieve at university. In interview and assessment centre debrief sessions I had seen and heard first-hand what employers were looking for from graduates.

At the time I had strong ambitions to work for a multinational upon graduation and pulled together a framework of things I wanted to gain experience in over the coming years. This framework was very much structured around knowledge and skills; i.e. what I wanted to know and be able to do. I felt it was important to learn about different business functions; such as HR, marketing, finance and IT as well as transferable skills in; communication, teamwork and leadership. It was pretty comprehensive; I put it together and attempted to log progress over the coming years. Honestly speaking I did not review it as much as I originally intended. I did, however, learn that creating this plan meant my mid-term aspirations were always at the back of my mind. In fact the experiences and achievements very much exceeded my expectations. I revised things, set new goals and achieved them.

When I look back, some of the things I am most proud of are;

— Travelling to conferences in Ireland, Canada, Romania, Germany, South Africa and Serbia.

— Chairing and training at leadership conferences in Germany (in both German and English).

— Running my own business for a summer in America.

— Elected to serve as Vice President on a National Committee in the Dominican Republic as well as a member of a Global People Development Taskforce.

— Achieving a 2i in German & Management Studies from the University of Leeds.

— Learning Spanish from scratch to fluent level in one year as well as the basic steps of Merengue, Salsa and Bachata.

Those five years were packed full of travel, adventure and learning. I really pushed myself; sometimes too hard and sometimes not enough. I will always look back with a great fondness of the amazing experiences and fantastic people I met. I was converted; a 5 Year Plan combined with a desire to achieve it had given me so much and so it is something I know I will continue to do for the rest of my life.

Writing and following my second 5 Year Plan has been a great learning experience. Interestingly the initial output of my second attempt was nowhere near as ambitious and stretching as my first. I had essentially sold myself short in terms of its timescales and things I wanted to achieve.

When I reviewed it 2-3 years later I realised I had achieved many things on the list. The remaining things could be achieved with very little extra thought or effort. Essentially I was sleep walking into achieving the things I had set out to achieve in terms of finances, career and health. When I realised this I set myself 3 stretch goals that I knew would really challenge me in the respect that I did not really think they would be possible.

As I write this I am coming to the end of this second 5 Year Plan. You reading this book will have meant that I will have completed two of my three stretch goals and if you heard me speak at an event before picking up this book I will have completed all three (incidentally the first one I set for myself was to buy a property and I achieved this a couple of years ago).

Whilst writing this book I have also been writing my third 5 Year Plan and my first 10 Year Plan. A couple of book ideas have been explored and drafted, but this has been an idea that once it hit me I knew it was the one that would be completed. Hopefully you have now got a better picture of how 5 Year Plans have helped me and I hope you will follow your interest through with intention.

Basic structure of an effective life plan

An effective life plan will consist of a series of goals that you want to achieve. It will have a defined starting point and a clear end goal. End goals should be ones that stretch you and therefore by nature need to be broken down into smaller and more manageable 'journey goals'. This is illustrated in the diagram below;

Journey goals are useful as a way to avoid becoming overwhelmed with the achievement of an ambitious end goal and an excellent way to keep you on track. In the case of a 5 Year Plan it is possible to align journey goals with the end of each year. The process of defining your end and journey goals will be covered later in this book.

How this book works

This book is written to be used as a guide to take you through the process of writing your own 5 Year Plan. It is practical book based upon my own 10-year study into the personal development field covering everything from goal-setting and the law of attraction through to the psychology of success and wealth creation. It starts with defining your starting point before moving onto the actual process of writing a 5 Year Plan. Although this is the ultimate aim of the book, it is full of ideas that will help you achieve the level of success you want to achieve.

After working through this book you should be able to do the following;

—   Understand the importance of a 5 Year Plan.

—   Be clear about your achievements to date.

—   Define your vision and values.

—   Write effective goals.

—   Write a 5 Year Plan that works for you.

—   Have the appropriate tools and ideas to maximise your likelihood of success.

Each chapter will have specific objectives and review questions to keep you thinking throughout the exploration of this area. To gain the most value from this book you should answer the review questions and complete the exercises. These are listed at the end of book for your convenience. Answering the review questions and completing the exercises are important because they help you to internalise the material presented.

When you truly understand and internalise information, you can then identify how it relates to you and your life. There will be some things in this book that may do nothing for you, whilst other things may quite literally blow your mind. Picking out the relevance to you will be the key to getting the most out of this book. Constantly asking yourself the question 'How does this apply to me?' could be something that helps you with this.

Ideas and resources that will help you

Your view of the personal development world may be positive, negative or indifferent. My view is that if it helps you to be as happy, healthy and successful as you can be, then it can only be a good thing. From experience of attending various courses and reading books I find that the biggest difference is made by actually taking action. This does not necessarily mean buying another book or attending a more expensive workshop! Instead it means identifying what you will start, stop and continue doing as a result of what you have learnt. Below are some suggestions to help you with this.

Firstly a strong recommendation is to use a notebook dedicated to the completion of the exercises in this book. It can also be used for jotting down any additional thoughts that may come into your head. You may have some 'ah ha' moments; sudden bolts of inspiration, powerful realisations or just some great ideas of things you could do differently. These thoughts can be like slippery eels; they can be easily lost if not captured through the process of writing them down. Likewise if you jot things on individual scraps of paper, then these can be lost. I have met so many successful people who practice the habit of collecting thoughts in a notebook. Surely if you want to be successful then it makes sense to do the things that successful people do?

The second resource that will help you will be the website accompanying this book – www.the5yearplan.co.uk. On the site you will have the ability to download templates for the creation of your own 5 Year Plan. As I write this I also have plans to develop other resources that could support you on the journey of writing your plan and help support you along the way. You are also more than welcome to e-mail your suggestions and ideas for resources that would help you (and others) with the creation and realisation of your own 5 Year Plan.

Finally I have included a list of useful resources at the back of the book. This is a collection of interesting books, websites, organisations and podcasts that have made a positive difference to me personally. They are things that I have personally used and I endorse based on my own experience. Even after about 10 years of studying this field, there is still plenty of great stuff out there that I have not even touched! Above all it is important to say that what works for me may not work for you and vice versa.

Therefore please feel free to explore this field for yourself, my hope is that I can give you a sound foundation from which to start.

Structure of book: Process of writing an effective 5 Year Plan

The structure of this book follows the 3 stage process of writing an effective 5 Year Plan;

1. Laying the foundations - creating the motivation for writing your plan.

2. Creating the plan - reviewing the past and present before planning your future.

3. Making it happen! - identifying the ways that you can make your plan come true.

The key principle behind this book is that you have ownership of how your 5 Year Plan is written and therefore you need to put the effort in to make it effective. Answering the questions posed throughout this book will move you forward. However what you do with the answers and how you pull them together will be the ultimate determination of your plan's effectiveness.

Before moving on to the nuts and bolts of working through this book, it is important to focus your mind on achieving a positive result from working through this book.

Exercise 1: Your best possible outcome

The first (and potentially most important) question you need to ask yourself is;

- What would be your best possible outcome from committing to reading and completing the exercises in this book?

Please take some time to think about and jot down your answer to this question.

If you are serious about writing your own 5 Year Plan you should not carry on reading until you have answered this question.

It could be anything from simply giving you some inspiration as to what you would like to achieve in the future, actually having a basic plan completed right the way through to what you feel having a plan will give you. Please be as detailed and as specific as possible. It may be useful to review and revise your answer to this question as you progress though the book. The purpose of this is to remind yourself of the commitment that you have made to yourself from picking up this book in the first place.

Checklist for success

An in-depth approach can seem daunting, so to ensure that you can monitor your progress I have also pulled together a checklist. This can be constantly reviewed throughout this book to ensure that you are on track for writing an effective and successful 5 Year Plan.

Do I know the importance of a 5 Year Plan?	Yes • No • Maybe
Am I committed to the process of writing my own 5 Year Plan?	Yes • No • Maybe
Do I know what my strengths are?	Yes • No • Maybe
Can I describe how balanced my lifestyle is?	Yes • No • Maybe
Do I know what my values are?	Yes • No • Maybe
Do I understand how my values influence my decisions and actions?	Yes • No • Maybe
Do I have a clear idea of where I want to be in 5 years time and beyond?	Yes • No • Maybe
Do I have a written list of goals in line with my vision and values?	Yes • No • Maybe
Do I know which people, resources and required for my 5 Year Plan?	Yes • No • Maybe
Do I have a set of tools and techniques that keep me on track?	Yes • No • Maybe

This introduction should have given you a better idea of the objectives behind this book, how it is structured and what you want this book to give you. It is now time to get started with the first part of laying the foundations for creating your very own 5 Year Plan.

The best day of your life is the one on which you decide your life is your own. No apologies or excuses. No one to lean on, rely on, or blame. The gift is yours—it is an amazing journey— and you alone are responsible for the quality of it. This is the day your life really begins.

— Bob Moawad

Part 1: Laying The Foundations
Why should you even have a 5 Year Plan?

Chapter objectives

—   To uncover how much priority you give to the important things.

—   To define a plan.

—   To explain the 3 reasons why a 5 Year Plan works.

Everything for a reason

We all do things for a reason; whether it is the way we spend our time, the places we go or the food we eat. Some of the reasons underlying these decisions will be purely emotional, others completely rational and the rest somewhere in between. Many experienced salespeople would argue that selling is a simple transference of feeling. This means that people make actual buying decisions purely on emotion (e.g. fear or greed) and then justify with logic (e.g. the product features or list of benefits).

With this assumption in mind, this book will cover the theory of the ideas around life-planning, but will look at the emotional aspects around planning your life. I mentioned at the start that ageing and death were two inevitabilities in life uniting us all. Another fundamental principle is that we all have the same 24 hours in a day and the 365 days in a year. The exact number of days we are on this planet is not fully in our control, yet what we actually choose to do in the time is something that the majority of us do have some form of control over. If we want to achieve a goal of some form, then we can choose to work towards it or not.

Imagine for a moment that you went to see your doctor tomorrow and that he told you that you only had one year of your life remaining. Would your perspective on life change? Would you end up cramming more into that year than you would normally? Quite possibly! For the majority of us as human beings we are comfortable with putting things off in order to stay in our comfort zone unless we are pushed to do otherwise. The forces that push us to change can be internal, external or a combination of these. Internal forces relate to the pressure we put on ourselves and external forces are those imposed on us by circumstances or other people. Which appeals most; telling yourself what you want to do, or being told what to do?

What is a plan?

A plan is something that can help us generate some internal force within ourselves. Developing this force inside can enable us to stretch ourselves, to grow and to develop as individuals. In turn this personal growth has the added benefit of making us stronger and more resistant to external pressures.

How do we define a plan? Research on the Cambridge online dictionary produced the following result;

> plan: noun (DECISION)
> — a set of decisions about how to do something in the future.

With this definition in mind, creating a 5 Year Plan for your life is simply making a series of decisions about what you would like to do. Is this something to be scared, excited or indifferent about?

There are 3 key and powerful reasons why you should follow through reading this book and put together your own 5 Year Plan.

1. You know where you are going

A plan gives you clarity and direction. Once a simple idea becomes ink on paper it is suddenly a physical entity. You have some form of map that can be referred to. If you lose your way you have something to come back to that helps you stay on track.

It is rare to leave our homes without an end destination in mind together with at least a rough idea of how we will get there.

There are some common things that most of us strive to achieve in life; happiness, to be loved and respected for who we are, attaching meaning to our lives as well as making an important contribution.

Maslow's psychological theory; the hierarchy of needs, states that once basic physiological and safety needs have been met, then we have a natural desire to achieve love and belongingness, esteem and self-actualisation needs. If you are fortunate enough to be educated to the level to be able to read this book, then the chances are that you are having your basic needs met. On this assumption you will probably be someone who is working to address your higher human needs.

The bottom line is that the people who have taken the time to describe how these things look and how they can become reality are more likely to achieve them. Simply put; you can't hit a target you can't see!

2. It's all about you

The strongest reason why anyone should have goals and some form of plan is because these things empower you. By stating what you want to achieve you are essentially saying you care about what you want to do with your life. At this point you are in charge and leading your own life, not someone else's.

If you don't have a plan of some description, then whose plan are you following? Is it your parents', your partner's or your friends'? The danger of going with the flow is that this flow may sometimes take you to places that conflict with your values and compromise your identity. We can become someone else and suddenly wake up one day asking 'where am I?' or even 'who am I?'. Having a plan of what you want to achieve helps you to define who you are and who you are not, where you want to go and where you do not.

3. Dreams come true

Not only does writing down what you want to achieve give you focus and ownership, it also increases the likelihood of these aspirations becoming reality. A written reminder helps you to keep on track; nudging you to take small actions that will make it happen.

You may recall Jonny Wilkinson's last gasp drop goal to win the Rugby World Cup for England in 2003. When interviewed after the event he said that the goal to win the Rugby World Cup was something he had written down when he was younger. He kept this end goal in mind as he invested hours upon hours of time into training. This defined goal combined with a perfected kicking technique meant that when he received that ball there was only going to be one outcome.

The bottom line

In summary having a 5 Year Plan gives you clarity and direction, helps define what you want and means that these things are more likely to happen. The subtitle of this book is 'Helping you to do the things you've always wanted to do'. The reason for this is that when you put your mind to it, many things are possible in a 5 year period. Central to the argument for having a 5 Year Plan is that it is a tool to assist you with actually doing the things you want to do. It is *not* about saying you have one to impress others! If it's that clear and simple; then why doesn't everyone do it? This is a question that requires further exploration.

Chapter 1 review questions

- What are the things that you've really wanted to do, but never got round to doing?

- Whose plan are you really following?

- What experience do you have of writing down goals?

No one ever excused their way to success.

— Dave Del Dotto

The reasons why people don't write a 5 Year Plan

Chapter objectives

—   To discuss the general feelings about 5 Year Plans.

—   To analyse the 7 areas that stop people planning.

—   To decide upon your next step.

Reasons or excuses?

There are 3 compelling reasons why a 5 Year Plan is a good idea. For many people not to have one, it is possible that there could be more reasons not to have one. The question to be asked here is; what's more important – the quantity or the quality of the reasons?

When quizzing a few friends about this area, there were responses such as "I don't know how to write one", "I don't want to restrict myself", or "I don't want to be disappointed". These are areas that I will address in the next chapter through looking at the mistakes that can be made. In this chapter I've categorised the various responses I have received into 7 different areas.

You may be able to add more and by all means have fun with that! At the same I will challenge you to ask yourself whether any of these reasons outweigh you being in charge, having clarity and making your dreams come true.

1. Cynicism

"That won't work!", "This is all head in the clouds stuff", "I'm happy with how I am, thank you!" and "That's for other people, not me!" come from our close friend Cynicism. The Cynic within us is an interesting character; very much a 'Mr/Ms Know It All' and he/she is incredibly gifted, because when we listen to them incredibly they are always right!

There are probably plenty more cynical reasons for not completing your own 5 Year Plan. By all means feel free to list them if you feel that helps, but again challenge how much weight these reasons carry and what's most important to you.

2. Fear

"What happens if it doesn't come true?" or even "What happens if it does come true?". Both of these questions can be tied into the underlying reason of fear. Although once written and answered rationally they seem to be trivial questions, their power in preventing people from putting pen to paper should not be underestimated.

Your answers may be slightly different, but in simplistic terms the answer to the first question is that nothing will happen if your plan doesn't come true and you will be leading your dream life if it does come true. On this basis you have little to lose and everything to gain. Using this risk-free assumption it is worthwhile considering how you respond to failure, change and how much you really value yourself. The motivational speaker Zig Ziglar says "Failure is an event, not a person".

3. Confidence

"I can't do that!", "That's what successful people do!" or "I'm a failure, there's no point in trying!" Anything along those lines immediately relates to confidence. The bottom line is that we wouldn't be human if at some point in our lives we didn't doubt ourselves.

If you study the lives of some of the most successful individuals they all had confidence issues in some shape or form. Former US President John F Kennedy spent a huge chunk of his life proving his worth to his parents in the shadow of his older brother Joseph Patrick Jr. His father had proclaimed that it was Joseph who was going to be the President of the United States. In her autobiography; Black, White & Gold, double gold medal winner Dame Kelly Holmes described herself as someone who is only really confident when with close friends and family.

Confidence is, however, extremely important in achieving goals. Therefore it is imperative you know what things boost your confidence and to find out what does if you don't already know.

4. Ability

"I don't know where to start!" is a phrase relating to the ability to write a plan. Your formal education may have been different, but for me personally at no point during school, college or university was I taught how to write goals or make life plans. I uncovered these things partly through accident rather than intention. At the same time these are two things that have probably made the most significant difference in my life. Therefore the vast majority of us have very good excuse not to write goals or a 5 Year Plan because quite simply we've never been shown how to do this effectively.

Having said that, there are plenty of things that we were never taught at school that we have learnt from life as independent adults. The bottom line is that if learning something is important enough, then we will learn to do it no matter what.

5. Vision

"I don't know what I want!" or "I don't want to limit myself!" are in relation to self-awareness feeding back to the fundamental question of "who am I?" This is often seen as a very fluffy concept, maybe requiring at least 10 weeks of Meditation in rural India to come anywhere close. You may have done that, have aspirations to do it or laugh at the very thought. Whichever opinion you hold, knowing who you are and what's most important to you can be extremely useful in formulating plans and goals that you actually want to achieve.

The concept of limiting yourself is an interesting one because naturally our circumstances change, we grow and we re-examine what's important to us. Although it will be covered later I will say that any plans you create CAN be changed! In my second 5 Year Plan I found myself almost sleep-walking into achieving most of the goals set. I also found that some were maybe not as important as I thought they were when I set them originally. The fact that this book actually exists and has been completed at the time it was is a perfect example of how goals can be changed with interesting results.

6. Time

"I don't have time for this!" This is probably one of our favourite excuses. The time element is quite often a big barrier for many of us. Work, family, friends, household chores etc mean that we are all very busy people. We are also bombarded with information and messages from a huge array of media. It's little wonder that we can't find the time to sit down and reflect about where we want to be 5 years in the future. We may recognise the importance, but the demands and pressures of our environment can constantly fill our time with distractions. That said I challenge you to consider how much time you spend thinking about where to go and what to do during a 2-week holiday. I then challenge you further to compare that time to the time spent planning what you do in the other 50 weeks of a year and indeed the rest of your life.

Have you ever noticed that when you get to the end of the day it is rare that you tick everything off your to-do list for that particular day? At the same time have you found yourself settling for second best when it comes to long-term progression? Many of us have a tendency to overestimate what we achieve in a day, yet we often underestimate what we feel we can achieve in a period of 5 or more years.

7. Paradox of planning

For many the concept of planning is simply a paradox. Many of us are aware of the need to plan; 'Fail to plan, plan to fail' is often quoted. This is completely contradicted by the apparent impracticality of planning. There are often things that happen to us on a daily basis over which with have little or no influence. There are plenty of external circumstances that we simply cannot control. These external circumstances can influence the thoughts and actions of others as well as ourselves. When life throws so much at us that cannot be controlled, then it can be easy to ask what is the point of planning. At the same time there are people that tackled external circumstances head on and made things happen regardless. Did Lance Armstrong plan to get cancer? How did he respond? Did Al Gore plan to lose the US Presidential Election? How did he respond? Did Dame Kelly Holmes plan to fail her Army Physical Training Instructor selection course? And how did she respond? In these and other cases there are people that have used negative and uncontrollable external circumstances to their advantage. The essence is that they have created new plans that have probably taken them on to bigger and better things.

The choice is yours!

The wonderful thing about life is that we make our own choices. Every day we can choose to be dependent or independent, to believe or not to believe, to speak or to listen. You've had the chance to have a look at the arguments why I feel a 5 Year Plan is a great thing and also why people don't write them.

You may have agreed with some, all or none of what I've said and that's great too. Even at this point you may feel that your time spent reading this book has not been worthwhile and then you have the chance to put it on your bookshelf, sell it on eBay or give it to a friend. If this is the case, then I wish you the best of success, health and happiness in whatever you choose to do.

For most of you I hope that at least some of these ideas have resonated with you and that you will continue reading this book. Especially now that you are coming to the part where you will actually be starting to write your own 5 Year Plan. Before we start putting pen to paper, I felt it would be useful to learn from the mistakes that can easily be made when writing a 5 Year Plan.

Chapter 2 review questions

— How much time or effort have you invested in planning your future?

— What's the real reason that you have not written a 5 Year Plan?

— On a scale of 1-10, how important is your future to you?

A page for your thoughts...

If I had to live my life again I'd make the same mistakes only sooner.

— Tallulah Bankhead

The mistakes that can be made

Chapter objectives

— To expose the lack of formal education surrounding life planning.

— To present 4 mistakes that can be made.

— To prepare you for starting your 5 Year Plan.

Life planning at school?

As said in the previous chapter; at no point did I take a class at school or university called 'How to Set Goals' or 'How to Create a 5 Year Plan'. Consequently I had to feel my own way through this process of creating documents that would ultimately shape the direction of my life. I've read books, gone to conferences and attended seminars which have taught me so much about this area. Learning and doing are of course two different things; therefore I found the most value came in applying these things I had learnt with great results.

The 4 Mistakes

To help you with the process of writing your first 5 Year Plan I feel it may be helpful to share the mistakes that I have made for you to learn from. These mistakes may also help to explain why previous attempts have not worked or why you have not pursued this process further. Looking back I can see there were four mistakes that I have encountered in previous attempts of writing my 5 Year Plans.

1. Poorly written goals

The most apparent thing I found was that I was not writing goals in a way that would push or help me. Some goals were simple lists of tasks and actions whilst others were so vague there was no way of knowing whether or not they were achieved. Later in this book I will give you a useful template to help you set goals effectively.

2. Lack of self-awareness

Where you want to go (your vision), and what's most important to you (your values) are key elements of being self-aware. If your plan is not in line with both of these things, then you will often resist the need to take action towards achieving your goals. Creating your vision and identifying your values will also be covered later in the book.

3. Not setting the appropriate level of ambition

This is probably the trickiest mistake to overcome. As said before we overestimate what we can do in a day yet we underestimate what can achieve in a 5 year period. Quite often your first 5 Year Plan may not be ambitious enough, although it is possible to be too ambitious.

I was extremely lucky with my first 5 Year Plan – it was ambitious and really stretched me, yet my second one was not ambitious enough. This mistake can be rectified by looking at the solutions to the other potential mistakes. Better-written goals, clarifying vision and values as well as regularly fine-tuning the plan can help you to get the level of ambition just right.

4. Lack of review and revision

It is quite possible that you either achieve everything with time to spare or that you struggle to make any form of progress. If the thought of being tied down to your plans is a big concern, then the good news is that things can be changed. The biggest benefit of having goals is that they give you focus and direction. Having said that, if you feel that the goals you set for yourself are no longer important or necessary, then you can choose what to do with them. Changing them on a daily basis may defeat the point of having a long term plan, but goal refinement is a useful strategy. There can also be a great deal to be said in stretching yourself through new or more ambitious goals, so long as they do not spread you too thin or compromise yourself as an individual. In some cases you may feel that you have been working towards someone else's goals for you and not your own!

Reviewing your goals regularly can also be useful as a simple reminder to make sure you are working on the right things. If you are not, then there is scope to think of solutions that allow you to dedicate your time to the things that are most important to you.

Are YOU ready?

So we've looked at the reasons for and against writing a 5 Year Plan as well as the mistake that can be made. This book is designed to help you to avoid making too many mistakes when you write your plan. With this in mind I think it's about time that we got stuck in and help you to write your first 5 Year Plan, don't you?

Chapter 3 review questions

—   What goals have you successfully set for yourself in the past?

—   How clear are you about where you are going?

—   How will you know whether your plan is too ambitious or not ambitious enough?

A page for your thoughts...

*The common denominator of success...
the secret of success of every person
who has ever been successful... lies in
the fact they formed the habit of doing
things that failures don't like to do.*

— Albert E. N. Gray

Committing to the process.

Chapter objectives

- — To share the lessons from the best.

- — To explain the concepts of self-doubt and comfort zone.

- — To find ways to create more time, luck and commitment.

What successful people say

In the years that I have studied, observed and spoken to successful people from the past, present (and future). When dissecting their advice they all seem to say pretty much the same thing. Examples of common messages are;

- — "Work out what you want and follow your dream"

- — "Believe in yourself"

- — "Never give up"

- — "Do what you feel passionate about"

- — "Keep a positive attitude"

- — "Stay focused"

- — "Work towards your goal one step at a time"

- — "See problems as challenges to be overcome and not as obstacles that stop you"

There are plenty of variations on these themes and there may be things that are not covered, but the above are the most common and by no means rocket science! If achieving success really is this simple, then why do a significant number of people not consider themselves successful?

You may or may not be somebody who feels you are successful. Regardless of where you see yourself now, it is likely you have doubted your own ability at some point to achieve a goal you have set yourself. When this has happened an encouraging friend or family member, an inspirational book or a favourite piece of music may have been the small, but significant factor that kept you on course.

The irrationality of self-doubt

Self-doubt is an almost irrational concept that makes us human. There are people no different to us that have achieved amazing things. Therefore the simple difference between successful and unsuccessful people can be summarised as the ability to keep going. Sir Winston Churchill is famously quoted; "Success is the ability to go from one failure to another with no loss of enthusiasm." If it's that simple, then what causes us to give up? I've picked out the following examples as things that I've heard or personally said to myself;

—   "I don't have enough time"

—   "I'm too busy"

—   "I've never done that before"

—   "I'm not sure if I want to do this any longer"

—   "I'm too tired to do this now"

—   "Maybe I should try something else"

—   "Maybe it's not meant to be"

—   "This is the sort of thing that other people do"

— "I'm no good at this"

— "I'm too old/young to do this sort of thing"

You may recognise some of these thoughts or words from conversations that you've had with other people. Sometimes they can be useful as they can help to protect us from challenging situations that may take us way out of our comfort zone. Arguably they can also be the things that limit us fulfilling our full potential.

Which zone are you in?

There are three zones representing different behavioural states that you can operate in; comfort, stretch and panic. How these zones link together is illustrated in the diagram below.

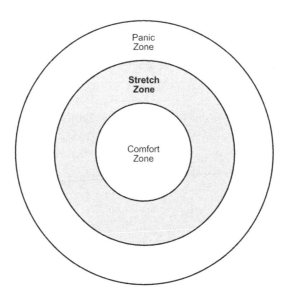

Being in our comfort zone very much relates to day-to-day activities that we can complete without much thought or exertion. This contrasts dramatically with the panic zone; where our body reacts to a situation that it feels is life-threatening. In between we have the stretch zone; a place where we feel challenged. Consequently this is the area in which we grow and develop. Interestingly the more time we spend out of our comfort zone, the larger it gets. In other words, if you do things that feel uncomfortable again and again, then eventually they will start to feel more comfortable. Riding a bike, learning to swim and starting to drive are experiences you may have had to demonstrate this point.

Ultimately the reason why we have a comfort zone is to protect us. The states that the body places us in when we are out of our comfort zone are a defence mechanism. These changes in state are part of our 'fight or flight' biological response to danger. Our evolution has meant that our perception of danger in day-to-day life has changed significantly in comparison to our ancestors. An example of this is how many of us fear speaking in public. To my knowledge no one has actually died from giving a presentation, yet it continues to be feared!

The ironic thing is that not stepping out of our comfort zone is something that can ultimately hold you back from achieving what you want to in life. As proved by the example of public speaking, these barriers can simply be limitations in our mind often caused by previous unpleasant experiences.

A story to illustrate is the one about a circus elephant chained as a baby to a metal pole on the fairground. Initially it tries with all its might to break free without success. After a while it gives up and assumes that it will never break free. Once this point is reached, a heavy chain can be replaced with a thin piece of rope and still have the same effect. Even though the elephant is now bigger and stronger, the self-inflicted mental barriers will continue to prevent it from breaking free. Experiments based on similar principles with fleas and pike have yielded similar results. This can also apply to us if we let it.

Writing, following and committing to your first 5 Year Plan may be something that takes you out of your comfort zone. To find the time to read this book and complete the exercises may mean you need to spend time by yourself away from friends and family, you may have to ask yourself and answer some difficult questions, you may have to watch less TV, you may need to get up earlier or stay up later. The list can probably go on further because everyday life can get in the way of this sort of activity. Not being fully committed to find this 'extra time' can probably be the biggest challenge that needs to be overcome. One of my favourite quotes from motivational speaker Zig Ziglar is "You don't have to be great to get started, but you have to get started to be great."

One of those things we cannot control

There are many things that we can change and influence in our own realities, yet the passing of time is not one of them. Time does share some similarities with money; when it is spent it is gone. The difference is that unlike buying something from a shop there are no 'time refunds'! A quote from the speaker Dr Topher Morrison that stood out for me at a seminar I attended was; "Time is precious and time is all we have." Although the passing of time is something that we have no control over, what we choose to do with our time is something we do have control over. If you recognised that time was the only resource you had, would you value it differently?

Why does time seem to speed up as you grow older?

The scary thing to note about the passing of time is that this seems to speed up as we get older. I've lost count of the number of times I've heard the phrase "where has this year gone?" Friends and family have come up with different explanations about why this is; whether it is becoming busier or having more control over how we spend our time. For me the best explanation of why the passing of time seems to speed up as we grow older is based on the relativity of time. If you take a chunk of time; such as a year, and proportion it to a person's age, then it will represent a smaller part of someone's life as they age. The table on the next page illustrates how much a year makes up someone's life depending on their age.

Unit of Time	Age In Years	Percentage of Life to Date
1 Year	2	50%
	4	25%
	10	10%
	20	5%
	30	3.3%
	40	2.5%
	50	2%
	60	1.7%
	70	1.4%
	80	1.3%

This effectively means that a year could seem to pass four times faster for a 40 year old than for a 10 year old.

On this basis it is important to think about what you do with your time and what's most important to you. If sitting back and settling for an easy and comfortable life is for you, then I will take no offence if you stop here. Although if you feel like you are going nowhere now, then in the future you could be going nowhere faster! The journey of developing as a person is one that involves an investment of effort and action to make progress. The point that I'm making is that your urgency to do things may increase as you age. It goes a long way to explain why people have a mid-life (and even a quarter-life) crisis. The speeding up of time has been so gradual that years have quite literally flown by.

How do you create more time?

With the realisation that time speeds up as we grow older you may automatically question where you are going to find the time to plan and do new things that you have not got round to doing.

It's easy to say you can do more, but the reality is that we all still have the same 24 hours in a day and 365 days in a year. You can't create more time, but you can prioritise where you spend your time. Completing the exercise below will be a way of assessing where you currently spend your time and how important these activities are to you.

Exercise 2: Where do you spend your time?

To prioritise the important activities, you first need to be aware of how you currently spend your time. Logging your time is the first step. You can break your day down to whichever unit of time you feel most comfortable with. Accountants and consultants who already log their time at work for the purpose of billing clients will have an advantage here. You may not want to break your entire day into 6-minute chunks, 30-minute slots may be enough to give you a rough idea of how you value your time. Ideally you need to conduct this activity for at least a week to be of any benefit.

Once you have collected your list of activities and tasks you can then ask yourself the following questions about each;

- On a scale of 1-10, how important was this to you?
- On a scale of 1-10, how urgently did this need to be completed?

Following an audit of your time you can subsequently start to place the activities into the matrix below that is commonly used as a time management tool. The quadrants have been numbered together with a general definition of the activity type as well as the nature of relationships and results.

	Urgent	Not Urgent
Important	Quadrant 1 Crisis Management Transactional Relationships Short-Term Results	Quadrant 2 Planning and Reviewing Fulfilling Relationships Long-Term Results
Not Important	Quadrant 3 Distractions Unproductive Relationships Wrong Results	Quadrant 4 Time Wasting Frustrating Relationships No Results

Looking at your completed quadrant you can ask yourself the following questions;

- What are the most important activities to you?
- In which quadrant are you spending the most time?
- In which quadrant would you like to invest more time?

Planning your life very much fits in Quadrant 2; something that is important, yet not urgent. Effective time management means that you invest as much time as possible working on the activities that bring you the most value. This also includes building the relationships that can help you achieve the things you want to achieve. The FranklinCovey Leadership Centre reports that high performance organisations will invest 65-80% of their time in Quadrant 2 activities compared to the 15% invested by typical organisations. You can't actually create more time, but consciously allocating time to work on the important and non-urgent things can help to save you time and make you more effective. Effectiveness in this case is doing the right things as opposed to efficiency which is doing things right.

Whilst completing this book I have started the process of implementing the David Allen Company's Getting Things Done methodology. I have found some of the tools extremely effective in recognising what commitments you have on your plate and how you can fulfil them.

If you find you are not investing enough time Quadrant 2 because the hustle and bustle of life get in the way, then you will need to commit to changing the way you manage your life. If you hope to do something new, then you need to stop doing something to compensate.

Exercise 3: Start, Stop, Continue

Simply by looking at how you currently spend your time, it may already be apparent that there is a lot of wasted time in the grand scheme of what you want to achieve life. The questions below can help you to reassess what you will do to change;

- What do you want to start doing?
- What do you want to stop doing?
- What do you want to continue doing?

Write 'STOP' or 'CONTINUE' by each of your current activities and create a list of new activities you would like to pursue under the heading 'START'. Assuming you are serious about following through with this book, you may want to add 'Working on your 5 Year Plan' to your list. This list can continue to evolve as you progress through this book.

How can you become luckier?

To define luck as sitting back and expecting everything to come to you without doing anything would be wonderful. Unfortunately having this actually become our reality is an illusional fantasy.

Many successful people do, however, explicitly claim to be lucky. On the surface it may seem to be true with these wonderful opportunities that were presented to them. If, however, you dig deeper, it soon becomes clear that these 'lucky' individuals have maximised their likelihood of succeeding through creating conducive circumstances. A speaker and author on the subject of wealth creation; Roger J Hamilton, defines luck in the following way;

Location	Being in the right place at the right time
Understanding	Being aware of external environments, and where opportunities lie.
Contacts	Knowing the right people to help you achieve what you want to achieve.
Knowledge	Having the right information and skills to make things happen.

Using this definition of luck can help us realise that even being lucky is actually a planned strategy. At a Houston Spencer's Life After Now Seminar, I learnt that although you cannot plan achievements with 100% accuracy, you can do things that maximise the likelihood of 'happy accidents'. Happy accidents are defined as those amazing opportunities that seem to land at our feet. Examples could be a last-minute invitation from a friend to travel to an amazing place or a call out of the blue from an old colleague offering you a fantastic job opportunity. In both cases these things did not just happen. You had a strong enough friendship for your friend to think of you and your former colleague trusted your ability enough to present an opportunity. It was the time that you had built in developing those relationships that ultimately created your luck.

The real motivator

So how do we build commitment? There are hundreds of tools out there, but the essence is uncovering your own personal significance for achieving a dream or goal. I heard a story about a middle aged man who had spent years trying to give up smoking without success. Smoking was already starting to affect his health; he'd digested all the scientific evidence, seen the stop smoking campaigns, tried the nicotine gum and nothing had worked. Then one day his teenage daughter stared into his eyes and said, "Dad, I want you see me in my wedding dress on my wedding day". The very next day he suddenly stopped. This is another example about how a simple, powerful and compelling argument can be something that radically changes the way we think and therefore behave. The man in question not only stopped smoking, but over the course of the next year he completely changed his lifestyle; ate healthily and started exercising on a regular basis.

There are a couple of powerful questioning tools that can be used to build your own personal commitment towards a goal that you set yourself.

Exercise 4: Focusing on the why

The first questioning tool is simply to ask the question 'why' and to keep asking it until you can go no further and have uncovered what is at the root of your motive. To establish and maintain commitment, it is critical that this is a strong and compelling reason. Repeatedly asking the question why is a way for you to justify something in your mind.

- Why do you want to write and work towards your 5 Year Plan?
- Why is that important to you?
- Why is that important to you?
- Why is that important to you?
- Etc, etc...

This activity has the most impact when you ask 'why' at least five times. You will know when it has been effective if you have stirred up some form of emotion inside.

This questioning tool is really useful for pinning down the ultimate reason for you wanting to write your 5 Year Plan and work towards the goals contained within it. The next questioning tool relates to looking at the consequences of writing, and indeed not writing, your own 5 Year Plan.

Exercise 5: The Cartesian Coordinates

The second questioning tool is referred to as the Cartesian Coordinates. This series of questions covers the consequential aspect of goal-setting and actions. The answers will be both positive and negative because the four questions leave no stone unturned in relation to your predicted outcomes. They are an especially powerful set of questions because they also get you to consider what could happen if you do nothing to work towards your goal.

- What will happen if you write your 5 Year Plan?
- What will happen if you don't write your 5 Year Plan?
- What won't happen if you do write your 5 Year Plan?
- What won't happen if you don't write your 5 Year Plan?

Ask yourself each of these questions in turn; remember to have fun and be patient with yourself when working through them. A couple of these can be real mind teasers! Once completed, reflect upon your answers and see what you think.

Time for some commitment!

Hopefully the process of analysing your time as well as uncovering your real motives has helped to create a sense of commitment before starting this fun and exciting process. Your level of commitment will ultimately be a critical factor in terms of how successful you are in following this process through. Taking the time out now to understand the personal significance is an important step to undertake; maintaining motivation and accountability will be something covered later.

Up till now I'm hoping that working through this book has been an informative process; that the information presented has been interesting and relevant, whilst the review questions have helped you to digest the information presented.

Once again I feel it is important to stress that the action you take, however, will make the biggest difference to you and your life. Consequently I would like you to take the opportunity now to block out time in your diary to work through the rest of this book. How much time you would like to invest is very much up to you, but the key thing is that you set time aside to work on creating your own 5 Year Plan. At the end of the day, your commitment will be your key to your success. The questions in the exercise below will help you to build a sense of commitment.

Exercise 6: Clarifying your commitment

The questions to clarify your commitment are;

- On a scale of 1-10, how committed are you to writing your 5 Year Plan? If less than 10, what can you do to raise your commitment?
- How much time are you willing to invest in the reading of this book and the creation of your 5 Year Plan?
- How much time can you definitely commit to on a regular basis to invest in the creation of your own 5 Year Plan?
- Who can help you with the completion of your 5 Year Plan?
- When is the best time for you to work on your 5 Year Plan?
- Where is the best place to work on your 5 Year Plan?
- What will you do to ensure that you follow through with completing your 5 Year Plan?
- What activity will you do less of to create the time required to write your 5 Year Plan?
- What will you do to remind yourself to follow through with the completion of your 5 Year Plan?

Once you have answered these questions I strongly recommend you take your diary and block out time in it to work on your 5 Year Plan. This simple act will maximise the likelihood of ensuring you follow through with your commitment.

Chapter 4 review questions

— What normally stops you from following through on the goals that you set for yourself?

— What can you do to address these obstacles?

— On a scale of 1-10, how committed are you to writing your 5 Year Plan? If less than 10, what can you do to raise your commitment?

Part 1 review

Have a look at the checklist for success and in particular notice your responses to and thoughts about the first two questions. If you cannot say 'yes' with absolute certainty, then I recommend you to reread the previous chapters and review your responses to the exercises.

Following this initial review, you can then ask yourself the questions below to help reinforce the learning taken from each of the chapters in this section.

— Why do you want to write your 5 Year Plan?

— What has stopped you from writing a 5 Year Plan?

— How will you avoid making mistakes in the writing of your 5 Year Plan?

— How will you make sure you follow through with the process of writing your own 5 Year Plan?

— What else have you learnt about yourself as a result of working through this section of the book?

Success is to be measured not so much by the position that one has reached in life... as by the obstacles which they have overcome while trying to succeed.

—Booker T Washington

Part 2: Creating The Plan
Acknowledging your success

Chapter objectives

— To stress the importance of past reflection.

— To draw out your successes with six key questions.

— To review your reflection.

Why even consider the past?

Before you start working out where you are heading it is important to reflect upon past achievements and learning. There are a couple of reasons for this. Firstly it helps to build a foundation that defines your starting point. Secondly it helps you to identify what is important to you and what is most likely to make you happy in the future.

There are six key questions that you need to ask yourself to help build a solid foundation upon which you can start to build your first 5 Year Plan.

— What are your greatest achievements?

— What are your defining moments?

— What does success mean to you?

— What are your strengths?

— What are your empowering beliefs?

— What are you most grateful for?

What are your greatest achievements?

We have all achieved something in our lives and it is imperative to realise this as it starts to create our own self-image as a successful one. The fact that you are alive today and have the ability to read this book are at least two things to get you started if you really cannot think of anything. Many people do not take the time to work out where they are going, yet the same people will often moan when they do not feel they are going anywhere!

It is valuable to consider all aspects of your life; work, health, relationships, travel, education, finances etc. In essence we are looking at your positive life experiences to date that have either involved you responding positively to a set of circumstances or making the effort to do something you've set out to do.

Exercise 7: Your greatest achievements

This is an exercise that involves you collecting a list of all the things you have achieved in your life to date. These could be anything from lucky breaks through to you taking on the world. Look to write at least 10 achievements here if at all possible. You may also like to rank your achievements to give you a clear idea of what you are most proud of. Some helpful questions for this are;

- Which involved the most challenging circumstances?
- Which were completely dependent on your own efforts?
- Which were achievements that you, and/or other people felt were impossible?

As with all the exercises in this book, make sure you have fun with this activity and try to get as much down on paper as possible.

Once you have your list of greatest achievements you can then move on to the other experiences that have been influential in shaping who you are today.

What are your defining moments?

The moments that define who you are today may be different to the successes and achievements of your past. Defining moments could be incidents that occurred before or as a result of these achievements. They may also be occurrences that have no connection with achievement; they may even be perceived as failures. The key things to focus on are the times that have changed your circumstances or attitude in some shape or form.

Exercise 8: Your defining moments

This activity gets you to think deeper about the experiences that have dramatically affected your life in some shape or form. Reviewing your list of achievements is a good starting point. You should aim to list a maximum of 10 defining moments in order to provide focus and clarity. Some questions to help you to identify your defining moments are;

- What are the boldest decisions you have made?
- What are the most powerful chance encounters and thought-provoking conversations you have experienced?
- What have been your lucky breaks?
- What have you tried that hasn't worked?
- Which seemingly negative situations ended up working out for the best?
- Which incidents could you refer to as 'life-changing'?
- What are your most memorable moments?
- Which people, books, films, plays, quotes, websites, pictures or songs have influenced you the most?

Once you have listed your defining moments, you may wish to rank them.

Once we have reflected upon achievements and significant moments we are now in a position to pull together our own personal definition of success.

What does success mean to you?

As stated at the beginning of the book, we are all different and therefore all have our own individual measures of success. When asking yourself this question you must constantly challenge whether these definitions of success are your own or whether they are other peoples'. Money, materialism and status are what people in many cultures aspire towards today. The worrying thing is that working towards achieving these may actually completely clash against our own values resulting in inner-conflict and unrest. It is especially important with this question to be extremely honest with yourself.

The benefit of being clear what success really means to you is that it helps to provide a basis upon which decisions can be made. This clarity not only assists you with what opportunities you should pursue, but also the ones you should not pursue!

The quotes below may also help to give you the inspiration towards the creation of your own definition.

"Success is the progressive realisation of a worthwhile goal or the pursuit of a worthy ideal."
— Earl Nightingale

"To laugh often and much.
To win the respect of intelligent people and the affection of children.
To earn the appreciation of honest critics and endure the betrayal of false friends.
To appreciate beauty.
To find the best in others.
To leave the world a bit better; whether by a healthy child, a garden patch or a redeemed social condition.
To know even one life has breathed easier, because you have lived.
This is to have succeeded."
— Ralph Waldo Emerson

Exercise 9: Your definition of success

This exercise aims to encourage you to get your personal aspirations out of your head and on to paper through working on creating your own definition of success. Your current definition may well be different to past ones and it may well change in the future. You can bring all these potential ideas from the past, present and future to create something that works for you today.

A simple way to stimulate thinking around your definition of success is to write individual words that you associate with the word 'success'.

You may like to take the words from your mindmap to create your own clear definition of personal success. Your definition could be a sentence, a paragraph, an icon or an image. The key thing is that your definition is owned by you.

Some deeper questions that can help you with your own personal definition of success are;

- When were you at your happiest?
- Who do you admire and respect?
- What sort of person do you want to be?
- What do you want to own?
- What is your ideal lifestyle?

With a clear idea of your achievements and definition of success you can move on to the next stage of uncovering the beliefs that have empowered and will empower you to be successful.

What are your strengths?

This question is commonly asked in interviews and often we respond with the answer of what we believe we are good at. This belief is frequently formed from what others have told us. Knowing what we are good at (and to this end what we are not good at) is extremely useful when planning what we want to do in the future. Surely it makes sense to focus on doing more of what we are good at?

Until fairly recently I would have completely agreed with this. This was until I heard an extract of a presentation by the motivational speaker; Marcus Buckingham, at the Leaders in London conference which altered my view on this. He argues that the vast majority of us are extremely vague and non-specific when we are asked to describe our strengths. On this basis he presented the case of a sad reality where the majority of us go through formal education and our careers without knowing where we can really make the biggest difference to society and the world. Marcus has a definition of a strength that really grabbed my attention. He defines a strength as an activity that makes you feel stronger after you have completed it. Conversely this defines a weakness as an activity that leaves you feeling weaker after you have completed it. For me this goes a long way to explain the things that we can do really well, but from which we receive no real satisfaction or pleasure thus leaving us feeling drained.

The second thing he noticed was that many of us describe our biggest strength as being 'good with people'. His point was that you if you feel your strength is being good with people, then you need to specify which people and in which form of interaction are you best with them. In other words are you best at negotiating, seeing potential, saving people money, selling to new customers, solving a last-minute crisis or another form of interaction?

Using these two principles of strength definition; identifying what gives you energy and what specific area of a task you are best at, then you will have much more clarity about what you can do to bring you more happiness and success. At the same time it means that you are the best judge of what your strengths are and not other people.

Exercise 10: Your real strengths

This exercise of defining your strengths is based on the above classification of a strength. Therefore you need to ask yourself the following questions;

- Which specific activities give you strength and energy through completing them?
- Which skills do you enjoy using the most?

Once you have these answers it might be useful to reflect on how much you have used, and are using, these abilities.

What are your empowering beliefs?

We all have beliefs of some shape or form and this is not limited only to those of a religious or spiritual nature. In this context we are looking at the opinions of ourselves and what we accept to be true. These may not be unconditionally proven, but there could be an emotional or spiritual underpinning that keeps us believing them to be true.

To this end we can have beliefs that either limit us or empower us. Since we are creating a foundation of strength you will need to focus on the beliefs that empower you. Empowering beliefs are those that help us to move forward towards achieving our goals and by this definition are positive.

Exercise 11: Your empowering beliefs

This exercise aims to bring out the things that you have believed or said to yourself in the past that have helped you to achieve what you have achieved. Some questions to ask yourself to uncover empowering beliefs are;

- What thoughts have helped me to achieve past successes?
- What positive qualities or behaviours do others notice I possess?
- What do I consider to be my strengths and hidden talents?
- What 'wise words' have I heard or read that I can identify with?
- What have been my most useful positive learning points?

You may find that the process of picking out your favourite beliefs is also useful as part of this activity.

Your empowering beliefs are ones that you can now take with you to give you the confidence to take action on the vision and plans that you set for yourself.

What are you most grateful for?

All too often we focus on what we do not have. The natural consequence of this is that we regularly have a 'feeling of lack'. This feeling can be both helpful and hindering. Looking to achieve something that is not present in our lives can be a powerful motivator; a reminder of a need we would like to fulfil. The danger is that if we focus too much on what we do not have it gives us reason to beat ourselves up. Regularly beating ourselves up can shake our confidence and stop us achieving what we want to do. The feeling that something is always missing can also threaten the one thing that many of us ultimately strive for; happiness.

Identifying what we are grateful for and reminding ourselves of these things on a regular basis can be a powerful tool. It can support us in the achievement of our goals; helping us when we encounter challenging situations or circumstances.

Exercise 12: Developing your sense of gratitude

This exercise requires you to list everything you are grateful for. If done correctly it will show you how much you have today. There will probably be things on this list that you do not really think about.

Some questions to help develop your sense of gratitude include;

- What positive things do I possess that can never be taken away from me?
- Whose love and support keeps me going?
- What are the positive experiences that I am thankful for?
- What opportunities are possible because of the life I am leading?
- What does my lifestyle give me that I have not really appreciated?
- What would I miss if it was taken away from me?

The list created by these questions may help you to recognise things in your life that you presently take for granted.

Staying positive about you

Through considering these six overriding questions in this chapter's exercises you should now be starting to build up a clearer picture of who you are and what's most important to you. Reviewing the answers to these questions may produce some interesting insights. The questions are focused on the positive, because drawing out your positive attributes will give you more strength and inspiration. The result is that no matter where you are now, there is some level of success that you can build on. Through completing this process you may notice some common themes which can help you with being able to set the direction you want to take.

Chapter 5 review questions

- What is your own personal definition of success?

- What are your greatest learning points so far in your life?

- What are you most grateful for?

Knowing others is intelligence;
knowing yourself is true wisdom.
Mastering others is strength; mastering
yourself is true power.

— Tao Te Ching

Describing the present

Chapter objectives

— To identify the most important areas of your life.

— To assess how well you are performing in each area of your life.

— To help you recognise where you need to dedicate more effort.

Where are you today?

Describing where you are today is the final thing to do before starting to actually write out your first 5 Year Plan. If you have not done so already, then I would strongly recommend you complete the exercises in the 'Acknowledging Success' Chapter. Once you have completed these exercises, you should have a clearer idea of your strengths and what you are grateful for.

An extremely effective tool for assessing where you are presently is the 'Wheel of Life'. It is effective because it gets you to look at your life holistically. The consequence is that it may help to explain why something may not feel quite right, even if on the surface all seems to be going well. Your career may be progressing well, yet you may be struggling to spend enough time with the people most important to you. Alternatively your home life could be fantastic, but it may be that you are not feeling valued in your workplace.

Exercise 13: Your wheel of life

There are four steps to completing this exercise in order to gain a full appreciation of where you are today.

1. Identify the important areas of your life

List 8 areas of your life that are most important to you. To get you started, think about the different roles you perform in your life, where you spend your time and what you enjoy doing. Examples include; Family, Career and Health.

2. Score each area of your life

Look at each area of your life and give it a score from 1-10 based on how you feel you are doing in that area; with 1 requiring the most improvement and 10 requiring the least.

1	5
2	6
3	7
4	8

In order to give yourself a fair score it may be worthwhile to jot down thoughts about the things that are happening in each aspect. There are three benefits for making the extra effort here. Firstly it helps you to recognise both what you are doing and what you are not doing. Secondly it may give you an indication of where your natural focus lies and where you are currently investing most of your time. Finally when you are creating your vision of where you would like to see yourself in five years time it helps to give you ideas about the direction you would like to take.

3. Draw your Wheel of Life

Draw or annotate the wheel on the opposite page by adding the areas of your life to each of the spokes. Take your scores and plot them at the appropriate points. You can then join the dots to see how balanced your life is.

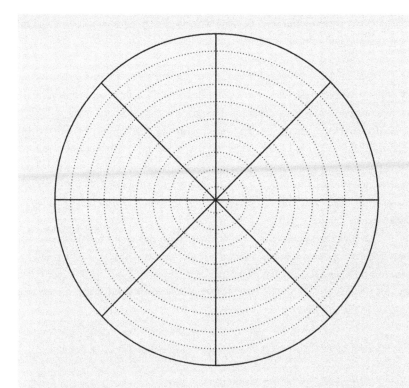

4. Notice the balance

Once you have joined the dots, you will have a picture of how balanced you consider your life to be. For each area you can ask the following questions to help you;

- What are the reasons for you giving this score to this particular area?
- How would you describe 10/10 in this area?

If you are serious about improving an area of your life, then the last question in this exercise is particularly important. It's perfectly acceptable to give an area of your life a low score; as recognising improvement is required is an important first step. The danger that we can get into is the acceptance that an area will remain a struggle indefinitely. This comes from not defining what the better situation will look like and the persistent reinforcement that having no direction gives you. It is really easy to justify something when we know no alternative.

One day I was waiting for a bus and couldn't help but overhear a conversation about how much one man didn't like his job. He complained about everything from the number of hours he was sat in front of the computer through to the number of times he needed to click his mouse (he had set up a mouse click counter because he was concerned about repetitive strain injury). He was moaning constantly to his friend for the next half-hour about everything he didn't want. At no point did he even mention what he did want or how he was going to improve his situation. Unless this attitude changes it is highly likely that he will still be in the same job complaining about the same (or new) things.

An important point to add is that your 10/10 definitions may change as you grow and develop. As you pull together and work towards your plan you may find you achieve 10/10 in some areas, but then may find there is more you want to achieve. The key thing is that you are setting your own standards for yourself and not measuring yourself against the expectations of others.

Laying the foundations before dreaming

From completing the exercises you should now have a clear picture of where you have come from and where you are presently. It is now time to work out what is most important to you. This will give you a strong foundation upon which you can start to build the vision of where you would like to be in five years time. All of your time and efforts will then be rewarded with the chance to dream!

Chapter 6 review questions

—   What are the most important areas of your life?

—   In which area(s) of your life are you performing particularly well?

—   Which area(s) of your life are you currently neglecting?

When your values are clear to you, making decisions becomes easier.

— Roy Disney

Valuing your values

Chapter objectives

— To define what values are.

— To illustrate how our values affect us on a daily basis.

— To help you identify your values.

The reason why we take action

One of the areas of personal development that I have found most fascinating, as well as relevant, to the process of setting and achieving goals is that of values. Whether we know it or not, the values that we hold govern pretty much all of our thoughts, words, actions and behaviour. They are an integral part of our personalities and can help to explain the relationships that we have with ourselves and others; both positive and negative.

As defined in Chapter 1 a plan is 'a set of decisions about how to do something in the future'. Therefore to ensure that you are making the right decisions and setting the right goals for yourself in your 5 Year Plan, you need to be clear about what values are and the significant influence they have on your life.

Values go a long way to explain whether you will choose to take action towards achieving the goals that you are setting for yourself. Whilst writing this book I have had a few informal conversations on this subject with various people and found that many are scared of not achieving the goals that they set for themselves. This can be linked to confidence as well as ability, but it can also relate to what is actually involved in achieving the goal.

Imagine, for example, that you had the goal to run a marathon, which would involve an intensive training schedule. This would probably mean spending more time away from friends and family or creating more free time taken from other parts of your life. The value you place on your time with friends and family or the other aspects of your life may be influential as to whether you follow through with this intention. With this in mind it is important to really clarify whether the goals you are setting for yourself are the right goals in the first place Identifying your own values is therefore a strong foundation upon which to set goals.

What is a value?

The dictionary definition of a value is 'the moral principle or accepted standards of a person or group'. As a definition this can seem a slightly fluffy and woolly concept. However when the concept of values is applied practically it can be extremely pragmatic as a decision-making tool. Stephen Covey refers to values as maps; a set of values being something that helps guide you through life. Working further with this definition means that having no clear idea of your values is the equivalent of having no map thus meaning you will struggle to reach your ideal (or indeed any) destination.

On this basis it means that if you follow the values of others, then it is feasible you may end up somewhere you don't want to go.

Being aware of your values is a key element of knowing who you are and this helps you to work out where you are going. One of the most pragmatic approaches to values I have discovered is that taken by Dr John Demartini. His definition of values revolves around them being an expression of your true identity; influencing your actions in such a way that you don't really have to think about them.

How values work

Values operate at a subconscious level that can go as far as dictating what you notice. How many times has a friend brought your attention to an item in a shop that you walked past without noticing? Have you ever heard yourself saying to a colleague; "It's so obvious, why don't they understand?" In the latter example there may be a knowledge issue, but the very root of this situation can be tracked back to what that individual has chosen to learn, study or focus on during the course of their life.

The filtering aspect of values is an extremely important one. We are constantly bombarded with information; around 2,000,000 bits of information per second. This is simply too much for us to consciously process. Therefore our internal filters (including values, attitudes and beliefs) will delete, distort and generalise this mass of information to 5-9 chunks. This tiny proportion of all that we sense then goes on to form our own internal map of reality. The phrase "positive things happen to positive people" is often proved true. The reason for this is that focusing on the positive means you are more likely to notice it.

What are your values?

You may have already uncovered your true values through completing the exercises in the previous chapters. The exercises so far have asked you to analyse how you spend your time and where you have focused your efforts so far in your life.

Using Demartini's definition of values there are some simple questions that you can ask yourself to uncover how your values are expressed in everyday life.

Exercise 14: Extracting your values

This exercise involves identifying your true values using questions selected from those created by Dr John Demartini.

Some of the questions in this exercise will have been partially answered in the previous chapters, so reviewing your answers should help you to identify your values based upon your actual actions. Ask yourself the following questions in relation to your present situation;

- How do you spend your time?
- How do you spend your money?
- How do you fill your space?
- What do you think about?
- What do you always have energy for?

Once you have looked at the answers to these questions, you are now in a better position to ask yourself;

- What are your top 5 values?

By answering these questions honestly and objectively, you can paint a good picture of how your values are expressed, possibly without you realising. You may find that your actions speak louder than words! When they contradict with where you aspire to be, the inner-conflict can result in a sense of emptiness and even helplessness. Understanding your own set of values can also go some way to explaining why you may not have achieved certain goals or procrastinated over certain tasks.

Do you own your values or someone else's?

Taking this further your values can also go on to explain your interactions with others. I am sure there have been instances where friends or family have told you what you 'should' do. In many ways this is very positive; having people care about you enough to offer their insights as to how you could solve an issue or dilemma you are facing. The danger of blindly following advice is that advice may be coming from a completely different set of values thus potentially compromising your identity. This explains why advice from different people may seem contradictory and also why a large number of people fall into jobs that they don't really enjoy.

Numbers quoted vary from source-to-source, but it is typically at least half of the working population who express dissatisfaction with their jobs. This is significant as it is an area of life that takes up so much of our time. I recognise that we all see our careers differently, but the reality is that this is something that consumes a huge amount of our time and is the predominant (or sole) source of our income. What you do in your career may also have implications for your relationships, self-esteem, health, lifestyle, leisure time and even your identity.

From personal experience of working with thousands of young people in the area of careers and goal-setting it is amazing how many base their aspirations solely upon their parents' aspirations. So many want to become doctors, lawyers and investment bankers because they are told they are 'good' jobs, but few question whether they would be the right job for them. This may seem obvious, but it is an issue that often carries through to adulthood and in many cases people are living a life that is based on the expectations of others.

Playing with your values

Through understanding the significance of values and identifying your true values based on your actions, you should now have a clearer idea of what's most important to you. Having a list of your top 5 values will be extremely useful in helping you to identify which goals are most relevant to you and which you will be most likely to achieve. If you feel your actual values do not reflect your aspirational values, then you will need to work harder at achieving the goals linked to aspirational values. The alternative is to phrase goals in a way that reflects your true values.

As you move on to creating the vision for your life asking yourself; 'what is most important?' can be extremely powerful. It is a helpful question for clarifying which goals are the ones you should pursue ahead of others. You can achieve anything you want in life, but only if you don't try to achieve everything. Values can help you distinguish between what is 'okay', 'good' and 'great' for you. Once you combine your values with your vision, you will find that creating your 5 Year Plan is simply a case of completing a jigsaw puzzle with the appropriate pieces.

Chapter 7 review questions

— What do you understand by the term 'value'?

— What are your top values?

— How can you align your goals with your values?

Vision is the art of seeing what is invisible to others.

— Jonathan Swift

Create the vision

Chapter objectives

— To explain the importance of vision.

— To define the two approaches to vision building.

— To equip you with tools and techniques to build your vision.

Why even bother with a vision?

Whenever we read or hear about successful people it is common that we discover they have a vision to work towards. Therefore the term 'vision' is prevalent in the world of personal development. The book and film 'The Secret' is an introduction to the concept of the 'law of attraction' and highlights the power of visualisation. Medal-winning athletes will hit nails into the walls of their accommodation before they compete to symbolise their intention. Successful directors will ask their executive teams 'what does success look like?' In Stephen Covey's book the 7 Habits of Highly Effective People; Habit 2 is defined as 'Begin with the End in Mind'. Raising your awareness to what you ultimately want to achieve during the course of your life is an effective tool for pulling together a 5 Year Plan. At the start of the book I presented the different types of goals; journey goals and end goals.

In your 5 Year Plan you may well have journey goals that lead to your end goal; the place you would like to be in five years' time. In the context of your life, the goals in your 5 Year Plan will, however, be journey goals. Your 5 Year Plan will be most effective after you have examined your values and created your vision for your life. This is because knowing your end goal means it is easier to know whether you are on course and moving in the right direction towards your ultimate success and happiness.

The holiday of your life

A way to illustrate this point is to imagine your life like a round-the-world tour. In this illustration certain countries or cities may represent particular milestones. Let's say over the course of your life you want to end up in Sydney, Australia and that you have identified San Francisco, Paris, Chicago, New York, Panama, Cape Town, Tokyo, Beijing and Caracas as places you would like to see before your final destination. If you were to fly to those destinations in that order you may struggle to fit them all in and waste a lot of time.

Revisiting places you have previously gone to may be possible, but may also cost you time, money and other resources at the expense of seeing the other places. Some routes may be more efficient and effective than others. Some people may help or hinder your travels and you may need to take different forms of transport.

Creating the big vision of where you want to be and what you want to have achieved is the equivalent of working out your final destination. Planning the most efficient route is the equivalent of planning your life. You are still free to visit other places, but travelling towards some places may mean that you are already closer to them. If you are flying from New York to San Francisco and decide you would prefer to visit Los Angeles, then with some minor adjustments you can easily make the detour. If on the other hand you are flying for the sake of flying, then you may find yourself getting lost and even running out of fuel in the middle of nowhere!

There may be some destinations that can only be visited at a certain time or age of your life, other destinations may be able to wait, some places might not appeal as much as others and other plans may change over time.

Again I stress; you can change things because you will change! On a practical level if you are someone who seems to change their mind from one day to the next then a useful exercise is to record these thoughts. Over time you may find that common themes develop; thus giving you something more specific to aim for. Additionally once you have a sizeable list you can start to identify the most attractive options.

The two approaches to long term planning

Long term planning can be an abstract concept for many people. In our day-to-day lives we often struggle to complete the long list of things on our daily to-do lists. When looking at planning for a longer period of time, we often settle for the security of the status quo. On this basis we overestimate what we can achieve in a day, yet underestimate what we can achieve in a lifetime.

So how do you go about creating your big vision? The best thing to do is have fun with this part. There are various tools and techniques that I have come across that are effective. There are two approaches to take and the right one for you may well depend on how you view time and the achievement of goals. I've categorised these as 'Visionary' and 'Tactician'. The table below gives you some things to consider about each type of person.

Visionary	Tactician
Focus on the end result	Focus on the next step
Struggle to define the first step	Struggle to define the end result
Like to pre-empt challenges	Like to respond to challenges
Perceived as 'fluffy'	Perceived as short-termist
Appear to be focused	Appear to be flexible

This table is here as a guide to help you to work out which vision-building tools could work best for you. If you consider yourself to be predominantly a visionary, then you may feel more comfortable imagining yourself at the end of your life looking back at your achievements. Alternatively if you consider yourself to be predominantly a tactician, then you may prefer to start with the present and work your way forwards; considering what you would like to achieve as you progress through life. By no means should you feel restricted to one type of exercise. Feel free to try both approaches and see whether they meet somewhere in the middle.

For each of these approaches there are a few exercises and some useful questions to stimulate your thinking. Have a look through the list and pick out what works best for you. Please feel free to mix and match; devising your own techniques if you are feeling creative.

Exercise 15: Looking back as a visionary

These exercises are most helpful if you are most inspired by having the end goal defined as a starting point to work towards. By their nature of projecting yourself to the end of your life (and beyond), the context of these exercises can be slightly morbid. It is therefore even more important to be in a positive state when completing any of these exercises. In each case the tone of the output should be upbeat and inspiring. A point to add is that these are in the context of you living your best possible life.

Looking back tool 1: Rocking chair test

'Something to tell the grandkids' is a phrase that sometimes gets chucked around every so often when talking about unique experiences you have enjoyed (or indeed suffered). This technique works on a similar principle. It requires you to imagine sitting on a rocking chair reflecting back on your life; recalling your most precious memories and life lessons. The questions below may help;

- What makes you smile?
- What makes you laugh out loud?
- Of what are you most proud?
- What gives you a warm feeling inside?
- What makes you feel satisfied?
- What still never ceases to amaze you about your life?

Looking back tool 2: Obituary

A chance to try out your journalistic flair. This exercise requires you stepping out of yourself and writing about your life as a neutral outsider reporting your significant achievements and events. For inspiration and guidance you may like to read biographies of people you admire or respect.

Looking back tool 3: Funeral

This exercise involves you describing your life by imagining how your nearest and dearest would describe you at your funeral. Think about who would be there, who would speak and what would they say about you. You can also consider how you would like the tone to be. Some questions to get you thinking are;

- What were your greatest achievements?
- What were your unique experiences?
- How have you lived your life?
- Who is most important to you?
- Who are you the most important to?
- What will you be remembered for?
- What would be your ultimate life lessons?

Exercise 16: Looking forward as a tactician

The following exercises will be more useful if you find an incremental, tactical or step-by-step approach to goal-setting more useful.

Looking forward tool 1: Vision board

If you liked collages at school, then you'll love this exercise! It will help you picture what your dream life would look like. Have a look for inspiring images from old magazines and the internet. Stick pictures that appeal to you onto a large board. The idea is to pull pictures from all areas of life and build a clear visual representation of where you are heading towards.

Looking forward tool 2: Mind map

This technique builds upon the earlier Wheel of Life activity by becoming more specific about the ideal scenario in each of the different elements of your life. You can draw your own images or add relevant words to describe how each part of your life looks, sounds and feels.

Looking forward tool 3: Life map

This is a tool that can look at your future in a more linear and progressive format. You can break down your life into decade chunks and name them (e.g. inspiring 30s, contributing 40s etc). Once you have mapped out your life you can add specific milestones that you would like to achieve in each decade.

Looking forward tool 4: Life list

A simple exercise is to list all the things you would like to achieve in your life. You may like to review, revise or prioritise the items on the list. Some questions to stimulate your thinking are;

- What are you building?
- What are the things you know you really should be doing?
- What would be the most exciting thing to do?
- If you only had a year left to live, what would you want to do?
- What have you always wanted to do, could still do, but have not done?

Looking forward tool 5: One year to live

This is a way to work out what goals are really important to you. Imagine that your doctor has diagnosed you with a rare fatal condition and given you only one year to live. You now have to decide what you would do in your last 12 months. It may be that you view things in a completely different light. You can challenge yourself further by limiting the amount of time you have to list the goals you would set for yourself or indeed the number of goals that you can list.

Crystallising the vision

Armed with these various tools and techniques you are now equipped to create your own vision. Feel free to be creative; mixing and matching ideas in order to create some physical representation of where you want to go. You could have anything from words on a page through to an annotated physical object. The key thing is that you are happy with the output and in a position to set more specific goals that will help make your vision come true.

Chapter 8 review questions

    —   What's your favourite approach to goal-setting?

    —   Which exercise(s) would help you most to create your vision?

    —   What are the things that absolutely have to be part of your vision?

Goals are dreams with deadlines.

— Diana Scharf Hunt

Steps to success

Chapter objectives

— To discuss the relationship between goals and success.

— To provide you with a template for setting effective goals.

— To help you break your goals down to the appropriate level.

Directions, goals and milestones

Once you have a clear idea of the direction you want to head in, you are in a position to formalise your plan through setting goals and identifying milestones. When you have answered the question 'what does success look like?' it is possible to identify the goals to be achieved. If you have taken a tactical approach to creating your vision, then you may already have identified some goals you would like to work towards. Whichever approach you have taken, writing clear goals is an important part of helping your dreams become reality. The process of writing goals down does not guarantee success, yet success cannot happen without writing goals.

The reasons for not writing goals are similar to those for not creating a 5 Year Plan. Unless you have been very fortunate, it is unlikely you have ever been taught how to set and write goals effectively. This seems strange, since the ability to set and focus on goals is a common trait that unites all successful people from the past and present.

The (in)famous Yale University goal-setting story

There is a fantastic story about a cohort of Yale University MBA Students in the 1950s who were surveyed about the setting of goals. The survey asked who had goals and then who wrote them down. About 90% had goals, but only 3% actually wrote these down. 30 years later the survey respondents were interviewed. The 3% that had written down goals collectively had an income that matched that of the remaining 97%. The interviews also reported higher levels of job satisfaction, health and happiness. This story is widely shared around the personal development field, although there are questions about its validity. Even if the story proves not to be true, it is still a feasible illustration of the effectiveness of goal setting.

How do you set effective goals?

The value of setting and writing down goals is that if done effectively it helps to focus the mind on ways to achieve the defined objective. Taking action to achieve your goals is the next step that makes achieving your goals possible. This chapter will hone down some goal-setting techniques that I have found to be effective. This starts with the 4P SMART checklist that builds upon the SMART model for goal-setting.

The 4P SMART Goal-setting Checklist on the next page is a template to help you to write goals in a way that gives you direction, clarity and inspiration.

Personal	Is your goal personal?	Yes • No • Maybe
	Do you use 'I' in the expression of the goal to make it your goal?	Yes • No • Maybe
Present	Is your goal written in the present tense?	Yes • No • Maybe
	Is your goal written as though you are achieving it?	Yes • No • Maybe
Positive	Is your goal phrased positively?	Yes • No • Maybe
	Is it helping you to move towards your intended outcome?	Yes • No • Maybe
Possible	Is your goal possible?	Yes • No • Maybe
	Do you feel it is achievable and within your control?	Yes • No • Maybe
Specific	Is your goal specific?	Yes • No • Maybe
	Is what you want to achieve expressed clearly and concisely?	Yes • No • Maybe
Measurable	Is your goal measurable?	Yes • No • Maybe
	Will you know when you have achieved your goal?	Yes • No • Maybe
Ambitious	Is your goal ambitious?	Yes • No • Maybe
	Does it motivate and inspire you?	Yes • No • Maybe
Relevant	Is your goal relevant to you as an individual?	Yes • No • Maybe
	Is it in line with your vision and values?	Yes • No • Maybe
Time-bound	Is your goal time-bound?	Yes • No • Maybe
	Does your goal have a deadline by which you would like to achieve it?	Yes • No • Maybe

A couple of things that make the difference

There are in particular a couple of things that maximise the likelihood of achieving a goal. These are; 1) writing as if the goal has been achieved and 2) ensuring that the goal should be written positively.

These two principles help you to create a sense of belief around a goal. One helpful thing is to identify the point at which you believe the goal will have been achieved. To refer back to the world trip metaphor; would achievement be the purchasing of the ticket, sitting on the plane or perhaps stepping out of the plane upon arrival? Clarifying the point at which the goal has been achieved helps with your focus and sense of accomplishment when it happens.

Believing something is possible is a massive step towards any goal you set for yourself. If you do not believe that something is possible before you even start, then you have almost given up before trying. Knowing you will give something your best shot is a good start, but believing something is possible with absolute certainty is one of the most powerful feelings you can attain.

The 80-1 shot challenge

I felt this sensation most strongly when I moved to London looking for work. This move was on the back of a year of unsuccessful job-hunting and with no clear idea of what I was looking for. I hatched a plan called the 80-1 Shot Challenge; the intention to speak to 80 organisations to discover what opportunities would be right for me. The aim was that in the process I would uncover my dream job. For a month I spent each day speaking to different people across London. I met friends of friends, people at networking events and even turned up at office receptions asking to speak to someone without an appointment. I remember waking up each morning with absolute certainly that my plan was going to work out. I shared the idea with friends and family; some got it and others didn't. Crucially something inside of me just knew my goal would be achieved regardless of what others thought. The outcome was that I found a job almost identical to the one I had defined earlier that year involving just under 80 interactions with different people from a wide variety of organisations.

Writing a goal 'as if'

When at a weekend seminar run by Christopher Howard I picked up an excellent format that can be used for goal-setting that helps you to set clearly defined goals based on NLP (Neuro-Linguistic Programming) principles. You may also find the below format useful to help you set your goals;

It is now _____ (date) and I am/have _____ (goal)

The funny thing about negatives

Writing goals positively is also important because the brain does not process negatives. The common way to illustrate this is to read the phrase below;

Whatever you do, do not think about a pink elephant!

What did you think of? A pink elephant perhaps? It is very hard or almost impossible to 'unthink' a thought that has entered our head. At the same time thoughts are extremely influential in how we talk and act. To achieve positive things in our life a good starting point is to phrase things in a positive way.

In the work I do with teenagers it is common that young people will talk about all the things that they don't want. Examples include "I don't want to get into trouble" and "I don't want to be late". All of these veer towards the undesired rather than the desired outcomes. Therefore it would make more sense to phrase these in the following way; "I want to behave maturely" and "I want to be on time".

Using this checklist and pointers you should now be in a position to write clearly defined goals that your mind can process effectively.

Identifying the milestones

Once you have clearly defined goals you can start the process of working out what needs to happen for them to be achieved. These are essentially the landmarks you need to pass on the way to your final destination; the journey goals leading up to your end goal. Let's say for example that one of your goals was to buy a property, then there are certain tasks that need to be completed before the end goal can be achieved.

End Goal:

—   It is 31st March 2012 and I am living in my own property.

Journey Goals:

—   Decide property location and selection criteria

—   Raise finances (deposit and mortgage)

—   Find suitable property

—   Have offer accepted

—   Organise legal aspects (solicitor, surveyor etc)

—   Sell or move out of current property

—   Organise housemoving logistics (removals, utilities etc)

—   Move into property

Identifying these milestones and attaching some dates to these is an excellent way to keep yourself on track and to create some form of regular accountability to your end goal. The process of breaking down a large goal into smaller chunks is another simple technique to help you believe your goal is possible. Once again I stress that if you believe your goal is possible, then you are more likely to achieve it. If you look at your list of milestones and consider them all to be simple tasks, then the goal has been broken down to the correct level.

Exercise 17: Writing your goals

Equipped with the principles of goal-setting together with templates means that this next exercise requires you start writing your goals. The key thing to bear in mind at all times is that the goals you set for yourself are also in line with your vision and values.

- What are the things that you have always wanted to do, could still do in the next 5 years, but have not done?
- What are the end goals that you want to achieve in the next 5 years?
- What are the journey goals that you need to accomplish in order to reach these end goals?

The template below may help you;

It is now _____ *(date) and I am/have* _____ *(goal)*

It is now _____ *(date) and I am/have* _____ *(goal)*

It is now _____ *(date) and I am/have* _____ *(goal)*

It is now _____ *(date) and I am/have* _____ *(goal)*

On the website – www.the5yearplan.co.uk – you will be able to download files that help you to structure your own plan.

Congratulations! Once you have completed your list of what you want to aim for in the next 5 years you have pretty much completed your plan. This also means you are well on the way to achieving your own personal definition of success for the next 5 years. The last part of the book is about clarifying the steps you need to take to make these things happen.

Chapter 9 review questions

— What's the value of writing down goals?

— What is essential to include when you write your goals?

— What 'Journey Goals' need to be achieved to help you achieve your vision for yourself?

Part 2 review

This is another opportunity to review the checklist for success at the beginning of the book. Once again the questions below build upon the learning you will have taken from each of the chapters in this section relating to the writing of your plan.

— When were you most successful?

— How balanced is your current lifestyle?

— What is most important to you?

— What is your vision for your life?

— What are the goals you would need to achieve in the next 5 years to help make your vision become reality?

— What else have you learnt about myself as a result of working through this section of the book?

You can have everything in life you want if you will just help enough people get what they want.

— Zig Ziglar

Part 3: Making It Happen
Mind the gap

Chapter objectives

—   To help you identify 'the gap'.

—   To define the three areas of the gap.

—   To provide suggestions with ways to bridge the gap.

What comes next?

By now your plan should be shaping up nicely. With clearly defined goals broken down into manageable chunks, the whole plan may seem a lot more feasible and achievable. At the same time there may be aspects that you are uncertain about. Doubting remarks such as "I don't know how to do this" or "I don't have enough time/money/contacts to do that" may come into your head.

Minding the gap is all about working out what supporting elements you may need to bring in to make your plan possible. There are 3 supporting elements that can help you; knowledge, people and resources.

Knowledge

Having the right skills, abilities and understanding of certain aspects of your plan may be crucial to achieving your goals. Knowing how to do something is empowering when you are looking to complete a certain task yourself. If it does not matter who completes the task, then a basic understanding may be enough. The phrase 'knowledge is power' can apply in each situation; from negotiating the best deal to doing the best job possible. In an information age there is no shortage of information out there to help you. To help steer you in the right direction there are the following avenues to explore;

—   Books

—   Newspapers

—   Magazines

—   Newsletters and e-zines

—   Websites and Blogs

—   DVDs

—   Audio CDs

—   Trade Shows and Events

—   Training Courses, Workshops and Seminars

—   Academic Qualifications

—   Trade Associations

—   Networking Events

—   Friends and Family

There may be other sources, because today's world gives us unprecedented access to the information that we need at the touch of a button. The danger is more that you reach information overload.

Exercise 18: Your learning plan

This exercise requires you to define exactly what you need to learn to achieve your end and journey goals established in your 5 Year Plan. Some questions to help keep you on track for this learning plan are;

- What exactly do you need to know to achieve your goal?
- What is the most effective way to learn about the relevant area?
- How do you learn best?
- What level of knowledge do you need to achieve my goal? Do you need to know how to do this or simply understand how it works?

People

People are social animals and so to ignore the importance (and at very least the influence) of other people in the achievement of your goals could cost you a lot of time and money.

Decisions made by others can affect your ability to achieve your goals. Additionally other people could have access to the skills, knowledge and resources required by you. Therefore the relationships you have with people within your network are a huge resource for you.

Your family, friends, colleagues (both past and present) and associates come together to form your network. I once heard that you should treat your network like an insurance policy; it will be there to support you in times of need, but only if you invest into it on a regular basis. This is looking at it with a survivor mentality, but viewing your network with an achiever mentality means that you not only look to maintain it but also to expand it.Technology today means that there are many different communication methods we can use to stay in touch with people. Face-to-face, phone, text, e-mail, social networking sites, fax and an old-fashioned letter mean that we can maintain contact with a greater number of people from across the world. With internet access and a mobile phone you also have instant access to pretty much anyone in your network.

When looking at your goals, there may be different types of people who can support you on your journey of achieving them.

—   Mentors; people who have already achieved what you want to achieve and you can call upon for advice.

—   Peers; people who are heading in a similar direction to you and have made similar progress.

—   Coaches; people who can be hired to help keep you accountable to yourself.

—   Connectors; people with large networks that can put you in touch with the right people.

—   Supporters; people who are positive and encouraging about you achieving your goals.

—   Critics; people who are sceptical of your plans.

A broad and balanced network with people that fulfil each of these roles will maximise your chances of achieving your goals. By analysing your current network you can see where your network is strong and where it needs to be strengthened. Analysis of your network also enables you to identify with whom you spend the most time. The people to be most weary of in this case are your critics. They can be highly effective in the role of keeping you grounded and being there to prove them wrong. At the same time if you take their criticisms too seriously it may affect your confidence and progress. These people may be close friends and family who are well intentioned, often looking to protect you from disappointment and failure. On the flipside their good intentions may protect you from success, so it is up to you as to how you handle these relationships in comparison to others.

Exercise 19: Establishing who is in your network

This exercise is about ascertaining who you know and where you feel they are in your network. The table below is an example of a format for capturing this information. Some people may show up in multiple categories and this is fine. The nature of relationship refers to how close you are to the individual in question as well as how frequent your contact with them is.

Category	Name	Nature of Relationship
Mentors		
Peers		
Coaches		
Connectors		
Supporters		
Critics		

Following completion of this table you can ask yourself;

- What do you notice about your network?
- In what way would you like to develop your network?

Once you have consolidated your present network, you can start to identify the type of people you would need to meet to assist you with the achievement of your goals. Your existing network will probably be able to help you out. The combination of modern technology and the plethora of events should enable you to track the necessary people down.

In Malcolm Gladwell's book; The Tipping Point, he presented the work of the psychologist Stanley Milgram. Milgram's experiment involved mailing a package to a named individual via a random sample of unconnected people. Through his experiment Milgram uncovered that we are typically five or six connections away from any specified individual. This led to the concept known as 'Six degrees of separation'. Human beings are all connected through a multitude of individual relationships. Therefore it is common that the people we would like to meet are closer to us than we think. Building relationships is the key to maintaining and then expanding your network.

Exercise 20: Expanding your network

Knowing the right people could make the difference between achieving your goals and not achieving them. With this is in mind the important questions to ask yourself in the context of your 5 Year Plan are;

- Who do you need to know?
- Who can help you get in touch with these people?
- How else could you meet these people?

Answering these questions should give you some ideas for next action steps to take.

Resources

The resources of time, money and specific objects are important to the achievement of goals, but arguably not as important as having access to the right contacts and knowledge. Your resourcefulness is the greatest asset you can have since it will enable you to access the right people in the right way at the right time. Whilst completing a programme with FranklinWaugh it was made clear that the acquisition of any resource is always underpinned by a relationship of some description.

Knowing how to manage your resources is, however, an imperative skill. Why do as many as 95% of new businesses fail within the first 5 years? How do Lottery winners end up broke soon after their cash windfalls? Resource management is something that needs to be addressed if you are serious about achieving your goals.

It all starts with how you manage your time. As stated previously, this is one resource that we all have the same amount of and cannot be reclaimed once spent. When you have decided that a goal is important enough to work towards it is down to you to prioritise and allocate time to dedicate efforts towards the achievement of that goal. Your plan is your reminder of where you want to go, but you also need to take action in order to make progress. The ability to distinguish between the important and the urgent is a key part of this as there is no shortage of distractions out there!

Next up comes money; something that makes a great servant, but is a poor master. With the right contacts and knowledge as well as the skill to manage it effectively you may find that this resource can go a lot further. Typically you will always spend what you have (and sometimes more!). Knowing how to save is a crucial skill for building reserves that you may require. The simplest way to do this is to pay yourself first; i.e. as soon as you receive your source of income. This means paying a certain chunk of money into a separate account that you do not access for day to day spending. Over the course of a year you will be amazed with the results (the level of amazement will of course be directly proportionate to your level of commitment and discipline). When looking at your goals you should be able to calculate the amount of financial resources required in order to create the necessary saving targets.

Why is it that so many of us aspire to be rich; yet so many fail to achieve that aim? Many people spend their entire lives working towards this aspiration without even deciding what to do with the money. Every so often we hear stories of misers who die lonely with huge fortunes acquired during their lifetimes.

Speakers and writers in the area of wealth creation make a clear distinction between the terms 'rich' and 'wealthy'. Roger J Hamilton describes being rich as the amount of money you have in your bank account whilst being wealthy is what you have if all your money was taken away. He goes on to define wealth on the basis of the equation of Wealth = Value x Leverage. The idea behind this is that making a positive difference to a large number of people helps you to achieve a high level of personal wealth.

Specific objects or possessions may be required to achieve a goal. Alternatively their acquisition may in fact be the goal itself. If, for example, one of your goals was a road-trip across America, then a car, bike or other form of transport would be required. You may decide to hire one or buy one to use, but either way it would be an important resource for the achievement of your goal. In some cases the necessary resources can be borrowed or sourced from trusted people within your network.

If you have set the acquirement of a particular object as your goal, then it may be worthwhile probing further for the reason why. Knowing the reason why has two benefits. Firstly it challenges how important acquiring this object is for you. Secondly the underlying reason is often a much more powerful motivator if known. Whether it is a new car, house or boat - it is useful to ask yourself; "what will this give me?"

Exercise 21: Creating your resource wish list

With clearly defined goals it becomes easier to work out exactly which resources you need to achieve them. If you don't know, then the chances are that someone out there does. The answers to the five questions below will be the final pieces in the puzzle.

- How much time do I need to dedicate to achieving the goals in my 5 Year Plan?
- How much money do I need to allocate to achieving the goals in my 5 Year Plan?
- Which specific objects do I need to acquire in order to complete the goals in my 5 Year Plan?
- How do I plan to acquire these resources?
- Which resources could I acquire at limited or no cost?

Congratulations! Once you have added this information to your plan, you will have completed your 5 Year Plan; what you want and how you will get it.

Are you a dreamer or a doer?

Identifying your gap is an essential part of making your plan happen. Working out what you can do to make your dreams come true will differentiate yourself from the dreamers of this world. It is great fun to think about the wonderful things you can do with your life. This can only be bettered by making them become a reality. Taking action is what makes this possible; something the next chapter will help you with.

Chapter 10 review questions

— What do you need to learn and how will you learn these things?

— Who can help you achieve my plan?

— What resources do you need and how can you acquire them?

Action may not always bring happiness; but there is no happiness without action.

— Benjamin Disraeli

Plan into action

Chapter objectives

— To warn of the danger of not taking action.

— To present five ways to help make things happen.

— To prepare you for starting your daring adventure.

Our limiting fear of failure

"I am scared I won't achieve the goals in my plan." From speaking to people about this subject, this seems to be the most common reason why people choose not to write a 5 Year Plan. This chapter is all about working out how you are going to convert your plan from words on paper into reality.

Before we go through some tools and techniques that can help you to stay on track it is first necessary to recognise how far you have come through completing the exercises in this book. By getting this far you have demonstrated a high level of commitment to yourself, your future and your overall happiness.

There is, however, a danger that you can put all this effort into working out what you want to do, yet fail to make it happen. I once met someone at a party who had a friend who was inspired by the film 'The Secret'. As mentioned before this is a great film (and book) to gain an awareness of the 'law of attraction' and the power of visualisation. This friend wanted to marry a lawyer and live in a New York apartment. She even had a clear picture of the apartment; there was exposed brickwork and a piano in the corner by a large bay window overlooking Manhattan.

To her credit she had got this part of the process bang on. The problem that this person explained was that her friend was not doing things that would help to make this dream come true. She had not defined why marrying a lawyer was so important!

Apparently this friend rarely went out and did not go to places where they could 'accidently on purpose' bump into lawyers. They also did not think that physically moving to New York would be a good idea to maximise the chances of making their dream become a reality. Looking in from the outside either of these possible options seem like common-sense strategies. It goes to show that we can be so caught up in our dreams that we forget to do the obvious things.

Already half-way there

Although this story does highlight the danger of planning and not acting, the simple process of writing a plan does mean that you are already half-way there. Really sitting down, reflecting and writing where you are and where you want to go helps to ingrain your desires into your subconscious mind. It is your subconscious that ultimately drives your behaviour.

Research by the Bernstein Centre for Computational Neuroscience in Berlin shows that your subconscious mind decides how you will choose to respond to a situation seconds before you consciously act. The gap between stimuli and response is what ultimately separates human beings from the remainder of the animal kingdom. Therefore what we feed our subconscious mind will significantly influence the direction our lives take.

Having a plan in line with your vision and values will automatically give your subconscious mind free reign to seek out all possible ways to achieve your goals in your environment. In simple terms, being clear what you want will mean you will notice things that help you achieve your goals.

Reminders

There are other things that you can do to maximise your likelihood of achieving your plan. Setting up ways to remind yourself of your plan can be extremely effective. Symbolic images, notes on the fridge or a goal card (template available on www.the5yearplan.co.uk) to carry with you, are just 3 ways that you can remind yourself of your plan on a regular basis. The rationale is that reinforcing your goals through visual cues is an easy way to give yourself a 'mental prod' to ensure you are keeping the end in mind with your day-to-day actions.

Fuelling the mind

There are similarities between your body and your mind. We should eat a balanced diet to have a healthy body and the same apples to the mind. A balanced 'mind diet' allows you to have a healthy mind. You can build belief and keep motivation levels high through feeding your mind with positive material. The information age means that there are libraries of podcasts, CDs, DVDs, youtube videos, websites, blogs and books full of positive information available at little or no cost. I have included my favourite rsources at the end of this book.

Being aware of the nature of information that you choose to absorb and how it affects your mood can be eye-opening. When I first moved to London and started commuting I used to enjoy reading a copy of a free newspaper on the tube before work. This was until one day I suddenly found that there were no papers available when I arrived at the station. This continued and initially I was disappointed; effectively suffering from withdrawal symptoms. After a couple of weeks I decided to invest in books that stimulated my thinking in a positive way; biographies of people I respected and books focusing around the area of personal growth. The difference was noticeable; I would arrive to work in a better mood than before with the input of attention grabbing headlines. The same applies to TV; I will feel drained if I watch 24-hour news channels or soap operas for long periods. As a test, check your mood after watching TV or reading the newspaper and see how you feel as a result of your response to the content.

There are also plenty of media forms out there that can make us laugh, inform us and inspire us. Whether you read newspapers or watch TV is your own individual choice. At the very least you should be aware of what messages you are voluntarily choosing to receive. Trashy or negative media can be viewed like junk food; it can be enjoyable, but too much of it and you will feel the negative consequences. The consequences of not discriminating the information you choose to receive could be negative thoughts, close mindedness or depression; are these really that appealing? And taking this one step further are those feelings ones that contribute to your happiness?

Creating accountability

How to create your own personal accountability very much depends on how you get things done. Setting aside time to review your goals on a regular basis alone may work for you. Alternatively you may find reporting to a partner, close friend, family member or colleague may give you the extra sense of accountability to follow your plan. You may find that the objectivity of a coach or a mentor gives you a new and helpful perspective. A combination of some or even all of these approaches may be required to ensure the achievement of your goals is kept very much at the forefront of your mind.

Celebrating success

Creating personal accountability can sound very serious and not that fun if you let it be that way. Building in incentives and rewards for reaching certain milestones can help you stay motivated. Anything from a favourite snack to a weekend away could be an effective focal point for you to work towards as recognition for your conscious effort. Again these personal rewards can be built into the reminders that you create for yourself.

Whilst at university I sold books door-to-door in America and met a girl who significantly increased her sales in comparison to the previous year. Her goal was to sell enough to pay for all her friends to come to Paris for her 21st Birthday. One of the things that she did was to have a picture of the Eiffel Tower next to her bed, so that when she woke up for a day's work she immediately knew what she was working towards. Being clear about how you will celebrate your achievements could be even more powerful than the achievement itself.

Your flexible friend!

Once again it is important to stress that you can be flexible and adjust your plan. Life is unpredictable; uncontrollable circumstances may be thrust upon you that could affect how you view things. The writing of a 5 Year Plan does not mean that it has to be set in stone. It is as much about reviewing who you are and what's important to you as it is to plan where you want to go. Therefore it should be viewed as a working document that changes and evolves as you change and evolve.

Exercise 22: Making your plan a reality

This final exercise involves clarifying how you will keep yourself on track to achieve the goals you have set out for yourself in your 5 Year Plan. Ask yourself the following;

- What will you do with your completed 5 Year Plan?
- How often will you review your 5 Year Plan?
- What will you do to keep yourself motivated?
- How will you remind yourself to focus on achieving your most important goals?
- What will you read and listen to?
- How will you create a sense of accountability?
- How will you celebrate your successes?
- Under which circumstances will it be appropriate to revise your goals in your plan?

The daring adventure

As we come to the end I would like to wish you the greatest of success, health and happiness as you write and pursue your plan. I will leave you with one of my favourite quotes that continues to inspire me to push myself each day.

"Security is almost a superstition. Avoiding danger is no safer in the long-run than outright exposure. Life is either a daring adventure or nothing."
— *Helen Keller*

Chapter 11 review questions

— How will you remind yourself to work towards your goals in your plan?

— How will you keep yourself motivated and accountable to your plan?

— How do you plan to celebrate your achievements along the way?

Part 3 review

If you have completed the exercises in this book, then you should be in a position to tick off each of the aspects that make up the checklist for success at the beginning of the book. The review questions below will consolidate your learning from the last section and help you to make the transition from the process of writing your plan through to taking action and moving forward towards its achievement.

—   How will you bridge your gap to achieving your 5 Year Plan?

—   What will you do to make your 5 Year Plan happen?

—   What else have I learnt about myself as a result of working through this section of the book?

Life should not be measured by the number of breaths we take, but by the moments that take our breath away.

— George Carlin

Epilogue:
The things you have always wanted to do

The end and the beginning of the journey

When you were young I am sure you must have had childhood dreams; those things you wanted to be when you were 'grown up'. It might have been to become a footballer, a singer or a dancer. Then as you progressed through your childhood you may have lost sight of your dreams. These dreams may have been left back in the past as you slowly decided that you weren't worthy of completing them or that they were too 'childish'.

It was late one night at the age of about 16 that I first thought about the idea of writing a book. I never shared this dream; only making some notes about the outline of a psychological thriller. It went no further; I pretty much dismissed the idea the next day. This was partly because I did not think the idea was good enough and partly because the thought of writing all those words seemed like a mammoth task.

After almost 14 years of entertaining the idea of writing a book, effectively 10 years of preparation, 3 years of starting, 3 book ideas and 5-6 months of actual commitment, my first book has been completed.

Why share this? Writing a book has been a dream of mine for years, yet it took me years to even get round to actually starting and then making this goal a reality. I can assure you that I have not been twiddling my thumbs for the past few years, procrastinating for procrastination's sake! It is one of those things that I have aspired to do for years yet not followed this intention with the bold first step and consistent effort towards achievement of the goal.

Are there any goals that come under this category in your case? Have you included them in your 5 Year Plan? Are the reasons for not pursuing them further genuine reasons or excuses? Please be honest with yourself!

I really hope that you have been honest with yourself whilst working through this book; answering the questions and digesting the answers. The reason is that this will be the only way that this book will help you make progress in your life. Everyday we meet people who are happy to settle for mediocrity in their lives; giving up on the things that will help to make them truly happy before they have even started. I hope you value your true happiness enough to escape mediocrity, to grow and pursue the things you truly want regardless of your background, circumstances, experiences or fears.

Writing your 5 Year Plan may be your first step; it can be the end of one journey and the beginning of an even better one – if you let it!

I will leave you with another one of my favourite quotes (slightly adapted to suit all audiences). I hope you enjoy exploring the recommended resources and find the planning templates from the website useful (www.the5yearplan.co.uk). Please feel free to get in touch to let me know of your successes or if there is anything I can do to help you on your journey of making your 5 Year Plan happen.

Remember to keep asking yourself; what is the one thing you have always wanted to do, could still do, but have not done?

James Mills

Our deepest fear

"Our deepest fear is not that we are inadequate.

Our deepest fear is that we are powerful beyond measure.

It is our light, not our darkness that most frightens us.

We ask ourselves, Who am I to be brilliant, gorgeous, talented, fabulous?

Actually, who are you not to be? You are a child of the Universe.

Your playing small does not serve the world.

There is nothing enlightened about shrinking so that other people won't feel
insecure around you.

We are all meant to shine, as children do.

We were born to make manifest the glory of the Universe that is within us.

It's not just in some of us; it's in everyone. And as we let our own light
shine, we unconsciously give other people permission to do the same.

As we are liberated from our own fear, our presence automatically liberates
others."

— *Marianne Williamson*

Anyone who stops learning is old,
whether at twenty or eighty. Anyone
who keeps learning stays young. The
greatest thing in life is to keep your
mind young.

— Henry Ford

Interesting Resources
Books, organisations, websites and podcasts

As mentioned earlier I have pulled together a list of resources (books, organisations, websites and podcasts) that I have personally used and found extremely helpful for my own personal and professional development as well as the writing of this book.

Books

Some of the books that I have found most interesting and useful for my life and the writing of this book are listed below.

The 7 Habits of Highly Effective People: Stephen R Covey
Self-leadership, values and principles, relationships

The 4-Hour Work Week: Timothy Ferriss
Entrepreneurship, prioritisation, lifestyle, creative thinking

The Heart of Love: Dr John Demartini
Values , relationships

Rich Dad Poor Dad: Robert Kyosaki
Entrepreneurship, wealth creation, financial capability

The Magic of Thinking Big: David Schwartz
Goal-setting, positive thinking, wealth creation

Wink and Grow Rich: Roger J Hamilton
Wealth creation

The Secret: Rhonda Byrne
Visualisation, law of attraction

NLP Workbook: Joseph Connor
Introduction to Neuro-Linguistic Programming (NLP) principles

What Color Is Your Parachute?: Richard N. Bolles
Defining dream job, job hunting

The Tipping Point: Malcolm Gladwell
Networking, social movements and spreading of ideas

Organisations

The organisations below are all ones that I have had association with during the course of my life to date. Through these organisations I have developed useful skills and met some incredible people.

Toastmasters International (www.toastmasters.org)
Toastmasters International is a non-profit educational organisation that teaches public speaking and leadership skills through a worldwide network of meeting locations.

Junior Chamber International (www.jci.cc)
JCI is an international non-profit organisation seeking to provide development opportunities that empower young people aged 18 to 40 to create positive change.

Pioneers of Change (www.pioneersofchange.net)
Pioneers of Change is an emerging global learning community of committed, young people in their 20's and 30's, from diverse cultural, social, and professional backgrounds.

AIESEC (www.aiesec.org)

AIESEC is an international student organisation that provides a platform enabling young people to explore and develop their leadership potential for them to have a positive impact in society.

Junior Achievement (www.ja.org)

JA Worldwide is dedicated to educating students about workforce readiness, entrepreneurship and financial literacy through experiential, hands-on programmes. Young Enterprise (www.young-enterprise.org.uk) is the UK member of JA Worldwide.

FranklinWaugh (www.franklinwaugh.com)

FranklinWaugh assists entrepreneurs with strategic planning and development of an optimised business model.

WYSE (www.wyse-ngo.org)

WYSE International is an educational charity that specializes in values and leadership education for young people.

Websites

Below are some websites that can provide inspiration, support and ideas.

The 5 Year Plan (www.the5yearplan.co.uk)

The website that accompanies this book. There will be further resources available to download that will help you write your very own 5 Year Plan.

LinkedIn (www.linkedin.com)

LinkedIn is an interconnected network of experienced professionals from around the world.

Meetup (www.meetup.com)

Meetup makes it possible for anyone to organise a local group or find one.

Quotes Daddy (www.quotesdaddy.com)

Over 1,000,000 famous quotes; I used this site extensively for the quotes in this book!

Podcasts

The following Podcasts are also a source of inspiration and ideas that can all be found through iTunes and downloaded for free.

Inspiring Words of Encouragement

Weekly motivation, inspiration and encouragement relating to business and personal life from motivational speaker Zig Ziglar.

TEDTalks

Audio and video from the best TED conference presentations with contributions from some of the world's leading thinkers.

Thinking for Business Success

Fortnightly podcast presenting practical steps to improve personal effectiveness through the development of thinking abilities.

David Allen Company Podcast

Podcasts on productivity and Getting Things Done ®

Made in the USA
Monee, IL
26 July 2021